BCPL and C

COMPUTER SCIENCE TEXTS

COMPUTER SCIENCE TEXTS

BCPL and C

GLYN EMERY

BLACKWELL SCIENTIFIC PUBLICATIONS

OXFORD   LONDON   EDINBURGH

BOSTON   PALO ALTO   MELBOURNE

© 1986 by
Blackwell Scientific Publications
Editorial Offices:
Osney Mead, Oxford, OX2 0EWL
8 John Street, London, WC1N 2ES
23 Ainslie Place, Edinburgh, EH3 6AJ
52 Beacon Street, Boston
  Massachusetts 02108, USA
667 Lytton Avenue, Palo Alto
  California 94301, USA
107 Barry Street, Carlton
  Victoria 3053, Australia

First published 1986

Phototypeset by
Oxford Computer Typesetting

Printed and bound in
Great Britain by Billings and Sons
Ltd, Worcester

Distributors

USA and Canada
  Blackwell Scientific Publications Inc
  P.O. Box 50009, Palo Alto
  California 94303

Australia
  Blackwell Scientific Publications
    (Australia) Pty Ltd
  107 Barry Street
  Carlton, Victoria 3053

British Library
Cataloguing in Publication Data

  BCPL and C.
  (Computer science texts)
  1. BCPL (Computer program language)
  I. Title
  005 13'3   QA76.73.B17

  ISBN 0-632-01607-8
  ISBN 0-632-01571-3 Pbk

Library of Congress
Cataloguing in Publication Data

Emery, Glyn.
  BCPL and C.

  (Computer science texts)
  Includes index.
  1. BCPL (Computer program language)
  2. C (Computer program language)
  I. Title.   II. Series.
  QA76.73.B38E44   1986
  005.13'3   86-23266
  ISBN 0-632-01607-8
  ISBN 0-632-01571-3 (pbk.)

Contents

Introduction

The CPL Heritage

The publication in 1963 of the revised Algol report [1] marked an enormous step forward in the design of programming languages. Probably the most important idea, which arose almost by accident, was that of *block structure* and the stack mechanism for implementing it. A block is a set of data definitions followed by a sequence of commands; and blocks may be nested one within another. Each data definition implies a *scope*, over which the defined item is "visible", i.e. may be legally referred to in either commands or other definitions. For definitions within blocks, the scope is the block itself. Outside this the item has no existence. Thus memory space need be allocated for data only while there are commands to process it; and data names can be reused in different contexts, possibly programmed by different people.

During the decade that followed the Algol report several new languages were devised, each claiming some superiority over Algol 60, but all borrowing ideas from it, including that of block structure. One of these was CPL (Combined Programming Language), which was a collaborative venture between the University of London Institute of Computer Science and the Cambridge University Mathematical Laboratory.

Some of the ideas that led to CPL will be found in [2]. It is described briefly in [3], and in more detail in [4] and [5]. It was never fully implemented, but it did appear on the Atlas computer in restricted form as CPL1 [6]. Today it is mainly of historical importance; and its interest derives from the fact that it led to the invention of a family of languages that have proved to be particularly suitable for system programming. The most important among these are BCPL, B and C. Many of the ideas of CPL have been included in these languages. Others have not, which is in some ways a pity because CPL introduced several interesting departures from the Algol 60 pattern.

The principal motivation for CPL was the contention that Algol 60, while it was an ideal medium for defining algorithms, was too far removed from the realities of computing hardware. It is probably this more than anything else that has led to the success of CPL as the progenitor of system-programming languages, which are nothing if not efficient in the generation of object code. The language's name, however, derives from the fact that it was originally intended, to a greater extent even than Algol, to provide a means for solving *all* types of problem, both numeric and non-numeric.

The basic data types in CPL are integer, real, complex and index, the idea of the last being to give the compiler the option to assign array indices and certain other quantities to registers for faster execution. There are also types Boolean (two valued) and logical (bit string). Compound types are confined to arrays and character strings. There are no pointer variables; but functions are provided to allow quantities of type logical to be used as list elements in the McCarthy sense [7], and thereby allow more complex structures to be built up. High precision types double, double complex, and long logical were also envisaged in the original design. Implicit conversion between one type and another occurs when both appear in the same expression, and if such conversions are meaningful. In particular, strings can be converted automatically to or from numeric types, though the compiler should issue a warning report whenever this might occur.

Expressions are for the most part the same as in Algol, though occasionally the syntax is slightly different. For example conditional expressions are given in the neater form

    e1 → e2, e3

which is preserved in BCPL and, with different symbols, in B and C. Several assembler-level manipulations such as shifts and mask operations are provided too. In CPL these take the form of built-in functions; though in BCPL, B and C they appear as operators. An interesting feature of CPL is that it permits the multiply operator to be omitted when identifiers consist of only one letter, thereby giving a program the apperance of "ordinary" algebra, thus

    bb − 4ac

This feature did not persist in CPL's successors.

The structure of CPL is essentially that of Algol, consisting as it does of blocks nested to an arbitrary depth. Variables are declared at the start of a block with the keyword let; for example

    let x be real

As in Algol, a variable is local to the block where it is declared, and global to any block declared within that block, where it may be used as a free variable. CPL differs from Algol, however, in that local variables can be initialised. This in turn requires the scope of definitions to be further refined from that of Algol to cover only the *succeeding* text within the block. In this way definitions can refer to earlier definitions in the same block to obtain initialisation values. Otherwise the Algol scoping rules are followed unchanged. The scope of a variable thus includes inner blocks except for any in which the same name has been redeclared for a new variable.

The simplest form of initialisation is by value, thus:

    let a, b = 20, t

a is assumed here to be of type integer, while b is of the same type as t, which should be a free variable at this point. Because b is initialised by value (indicated by the = symbol), it takes whatever value t possesses at the time when the declaration is elaborated. There is a second form of initialisation called initialisation by substitution. After the declaration

    let R ≡ Sqrt(xx + yy)

any appearance of R in an expression causes its value to be recalculated in terms of the values of x and y obtaining at the time. R thereby takes on some of the power of a function.

A third form of initialisation is by reference. The declaration

    p ≃ q

causes references to p to be interpreted as if they were references to q. Thus, not only does the value of p follow that of q throughout the block, but the value of q can be changed by an assignment to p. The facility to initialise local variables by reference makes it possible to achieve side-effects. Initialisation by substitution gives even more power, allowing the possibility of expressing some algorithms very succinctly (and sometimes quite incomprehensibly).

It is characteristic of CPL that it permits mathematical concepts to be expressed in a manner very close to the conventions of ordinary algebra. We have seen how the multiplication sign can be omitted when identifiers are single lower-case letters. CPL follows another common algebraic convention in providing a where clause, which permits local definitions to be added to commands, thus

    R1, R2 := s + t, s − t
    where { s = −b/2a and t = sqrt(bb − 4ac)/2a }

In this example, s and t are initialised within the where clause by value, though CPL also permits initialisation here by reference or substitution. where clauses are intended to bind free variables within a single expression, and thus provide something of the computing power of the lambda calculus [8].

Functions in CPL are similar to typed procedures in Algol. However, because of initialisation by substitution, the distinction between a variable and a function is blurred. Indeed the term *function variable* is used in the literature. Function variables, in contrast to ordinary variables, can always be parameterised. The three initialisation mechanisms by value, by reference and by substitution are extended in CPL to parameter passing as well. (Algol merely had by value and by substitution, or *by name*, to use the Algol term). Another departure from Algol is that recursive functions must be expressly declared as such in CPL. This, it was hoped, would lead to economies in the object code for non-recursive functions.

In most instances the body of a function is defined by a sequence of commands. In such cases the body itself is introduced by the keyword resultof, to give it the significance of an expression. In this case the function body must also contain at least one instance of the command

```
resultis E
```

where E is an expression using variables within the visible scope of the function body.

CPL was one of the first languages to require explicit typing of function and routine parameters, thus:

```
let real function integrate[real lower, upper, real function
[real] F] ≡ . . .
```

Strong type checking is regarded as essential by many authorities today, and its absence from C as a fault in that language.

Routine variables are like Algol non-typed procedures; but in CPL they may be passed, like function variables, as parameters of other functions or routines. This may not look very useful; but there are applications. One such might arise from the use of routines to return two or more results, thereby avoiding the single-value limitation of a function. For example

```
routine quadroots[real a, b, c, R1, R2]
ref R1, R2
{R1, R2 := s+t, s−t
where {s = −b/2a and t = Sqrt(bb − 4ac)/2a}
```

The parameters R1 and R2 here are passed by reference, so that the two roots can be passed back after the computed values have been assigned to them.

The array features of CPL are very flexible. In the basic array declaration nothing need be specified but the dimensionality, thus

```
let a be logical 3 array
```

Declaring the actual bounds is treated as initialising, and requires the use of a special system function, thus

```
let B = Newarray[integer(1,n),(−4,4)]
```

the first upper bound in this case being determined by a previously computed quantity. By using a different function, the elements of the array can be given initial values:

```
let P = Formarray[real(1,2),(1,2)][8, 10, −15.4, 3.1]
```

CPL has a richer set of command formats than Algol. Conditional commands are:

```
if b then do C
unless b then do C
test b then do C1 or do C2
```

where b is a Boolean expression and C, C1 and C2 represent a command (either simple or compound). There are four forms of indefinite loop:

```
while b do C
until b do C
C repeat while b
C repeat until b.
```

The syntax of the counting loop is

```
for v = step E1, E2, E3 do C
```

where v is the controlled variable, E1, E2 and E3 are arithmetic expressions, and C is a command. v is set initially to E1; and C is then obeyed repetitively, v being increased by E2 on each cycle until its value exceeds E3. A criticism of Algol was that all conditions of the counting loop were not precisely laid down. This mistake was not repeated in CPL. The control variable is *local* to the command, and ceases to exist on exit. Moreover the expressions E1, E2 and E3 are evaluated once for all at the start, so that a change in their values implied by assignments in C cannot alter the number of cycles.

BCPL

BCPL (Basic CPL) was devised by Martin Richards and implemented by him on CTSS at Project MAC at MIT in 1967. It was originally intended as a tool for writing compilers; so it leaves out those features of CPL that were intended primarily to assist in programming numerical algorithms. It was designed from the outset to allow for separate compilation; and to this end the concept of *global* data is introduced.

BCPL is essentially at a lower level than CPL. It is a typeless language, or, more properly, a language whose only type is the binary word. Moreover it incorporates several simplifications in comparison with CPL. For instance the CPL rule that the scope of a variable extends to inner blocks does not apply in BCPL. This enabled the BCPL control to dispense with the static display mechanism. To make it easier for procedures to communicate, the concept of *static* variables was introduced.

BCPL and its successors also omit some of the more powerful features of CPL, such as the where clause, and the various modes of initialisation and parameter passing. In expression and command format, BCPL generally follows the lead set by CPL; and it produces code that is nearly as compact as hand-coding. Information on its implementation, appears in [9]. There are also several texts on individual implementations, showing a variety of extensions to the language.

One of the features that makes BCPL and its successors particularly valuable for system programming is the provision of addressing operators that give the programmer access to the *left values* of variables, that is to the addresses that are associated with names or expressions appearing on the left-hand side of assignments. This feature did not appear in CPL because it is inherently "unsafe".

B

B was devised and implemented by Ritchie and Thompson at Bell Laboratories. It claims, like BCPL, to be typeless, despite the fact that it incorporates floating-point operations. It does this "typelessly", as do a number of extensions to BCPL, by providing a minimal set of floating-point operators in addition to those used for integers. Being typeless, it retains BCPL's simplicity in the compiler. It introduced several new ideas, and has been implemented on several mainframe machines; but it is chiefly of importance now as the forerunner of C.

C

C was designed by Dennis Ritchie as the programming language for UNIX. Although it has been implemented on other systems, it is chiefly to be thought of in connection with UNIX*, and it is principally so that we describe it here. It differs from B in having several genuine data types, both simple and compound. Although pointers are associated by the compiler with specific types, C cannot truly be said to be strongly typed, because the provision of address operators, combined with a reliance on the user to check the types of externals, makes it impossible to apply strong type checking throughout. However, UNIX provides a tool called lint, which can be used among other things to apply more stringent type checks. The nearest thing to an official definition of C is probably the book by Kernighan & Ritchie [10]; but UNIX implementations, in particular the widely used portable C compiler originally written for the Berkeley UNIX system, provide several extensions, particularly to the function library.

References

[1] Naur, P. (Ed.) Revised Report on the Algorithmic Language ALGOL 60, *The Computer Journal*, **5** (1963), p. 341.
[2] Strachey, C. and Wilkes, M.V. Some proposals for improving the efficiency of ALGOL 60, *Comm. ACM*, **4** (1961), p. 448.
[3] Barron D.W. *et al.* The main features of CPL, *The Computer Journal*, **6** (1963), p. 134.
[4] *CPL Elementary Programming Manual*, Cambridge University Math. Lab., March 1965.
[5] Strachey, C., CPL Working Papers, Cambridge University Math. Lab., 1965.
[6] Coulouris G.F. and Goodey T.J., *The CPL1 System Manual*, University of London Institute of Computer Science, March 1966.
[7] McCarthy, J. Recursive functions of symbolic expressions and their computation by machine, *Comm. ACM*, **3** (1960), p. 184.
[8] Church, A. *The Calculi of Lambda Conversion*. Princeton University Press, (1941).
[9] Richards, M. and Whitby-Strevens, C. *BCPL — The Language and its Compiler*. Cambridge University Press (1980).
[10] Kernighan B.W. and Ritchie D.M., *The C Programming Language*, Prentice-Hall (1978).
[11] Electronics, Oct 20, 1982, P. 108 (Article on Ritchie & Thompson)

---

*UNIX is a trademark of ITT Bell Laboratories.

Chapter 1

BCPL Structure and Declarations

A source program in BCPL, as in other programming languages, is a sequence of graphic (printable) symbols. This is treated by the compiler as a sequence of lexical atoms that may be reserved system words, identifiers, or items of literal data. Lexical items are normally separated from one another by spaces or newlines; but in BCPL they may be run together in cases where it would be obvious to a compiler where the break came.

By system words we mean operators or punctuation marks or sequences of symbols denoting single linguistic components. Identifiers are used to "name" the objects manipulated by the program. They are sequences of letters, digits and full stops, and must start with a letter. Some implementations allow the use of other symbols, such as the underline. Earlier implementations of BCPL accepted only capital letters. Later ones are case-independent.

Literal data items are integers, characters and strings. In BCPL an integer is taken to be in decimal radix, unless it is preceded by # or #O, when it is taken to be octal, or by #X, when it is hexadecimal.

A single character may be represented as a constant. To distinguish it from a single-letter identifier it is enclosed in single quotes. The value represented by it depends on the code used by the implementor, which is not necessarily ASCII. If ASCII were used, then 'A', #101, #X41 and 65 would be different representations of the same internal value. Although most implementations use ASCII, this cannot be guaranteed, so you should always use the 'quoted' form when referring to characters. The expression 'E' − 'A' should always yield the result 4 whatever codes are assigned to E and A. We shall deal with the representation of strings later on.

1.1 WORDS

BCPL was designed as a simplification of CPL; i.e. it was intended to yield a compiler that would operate faster, and in a smaller store, than one for CPL. Probably the most important simplification is that BCPL admits only a single data type, which is referred to as a *word*. In the original implementation the word had 16 bits. But modern addressing facilities demand numbers and addresses greater than 65535, so most implementations of BCPL today have a 32-bit word, which is what we shall be describing in this book.

A word occupies a single storage cell, and can represent at option an integer (signed number or unsigned memory address), a single truth value, a binary powerset, a sequence of (four) bytes, or a single character — this last being placed in its low-order byte with the remainder of the word set to zero. There are operators to handle words according to each of these interpretations. For instance

    a + b

gives a result in which a and b are both integers, while

    a & b

takes them to be either truth values or powersets. The shift-left operator in

    a << b

takes a as a binary string and b as an integer defining the number of places to shift.

1.2　RIGHT VALUES AND LEFT VALUES

In a simple assignment such as

    x := y

the identifiers x and y are treated differently. While y is evaluated to give the content of the cell associated with it, x is evaluated to yield the address of the cell itself, which is where a copy of the content of the y cell is to be placed. Since the way an identifier is used depends on whether it appears on the right or left of the assignment operator, we refer to identifiers as having both a *right value* and a *left value*.

In BCPL, both left value and right value are words; so they are the same length, and there is no reason why the left value of one identifier should not be the same as the right value of another. The second is then said to contain a *pointer* to the first. The situation might be represented diagrammatically as

　　　　　second　　　　　　　　　　　first

BCPL has a left-value operator that forces a variable on the right-hand side of an assignment to be evaluated to its left value. This usually uses the symbol @ ; but many systems provide LV as a synonym. The assignment

second := @ first

would assign the left value of first to second, and produce the situation shown in the diagram above. @ is known as the *address operator*. It can be applied legitimately only to something that can yield an address. This does not mean quite the same thing as something that can legitimately appear only on the left-hand side of an assignment, though it would be as nonsensical to write @(x + y) or @1234 as to put (x + y) or 1234 on the left of an assignment.

By symmetry, BCPL also provides a right-value operator. This is ! ; but a synonym RV can also be found. The assignment

third := ! second

would assign to third the value in the cell *pointed to* by second. If second had been given the value @ first as in the previous example, then the result would be the same as the assignment

third := first

! is known as the *contents* or *indirection* operator. It can be applied to any expression. The expression is evaluated, the result is interpreted as a left value, and the corresponding right value is returned as the value of the expression. This is sometimes known as *dereferencing*.

Expressions involving ! can appear on the left-hand side of an assignment. Thus

!x := 1234

assigns the number 1234 to the cell whose address is the right value associated with x. After the assignment we might show the situation diagrammatically thus:

Notice that the expression !x always treats the content of x as a pointer even if no pointer has actually been assigned to x. This is a fruitful source of error for novice BCPL programmers. During execution such an error is often trapped as a "bus error", i.e. an attempt to refer to a protected area of memory, or a memory location that is not physically present.

! is the inverse of the address operator, @. In other words, writing @!x or !@x is equivalent to writing simply x. @ and ! are both unary (monadic) operators requiring only one operand; but we shall see later that ! can have a dyadic function as well, so that a meaning can be ascribed to, say, x!y.

1.3 BLOCK STRUCTURE

BCPL follows CPL in being an Algol-like language. That is to say, source programs consist of one or more functional *blocks*, any of which may be enclosed within other blocks. When the flow of control enters a new block, a new activation record is created in the working area, which, following other block-structured languages, is a stack. When control exits from a block, the activation record is deleted from the stack; and control reverts to the activation record below it. The beginning of a block is denoted in BCPL by the symbol $(, and its end by the symbol $). $(and $) are known as *section brackets*.

Optionally section brackets may be followed imediately by a numeric or alphabetic tag. An opening section bracket is then to be matched with a closing bracket bearing the same tag. This means that, when several closing brackets are called for in sequence, only the last need appear; and it should be tagged to match the corresponding (first) opening bracket. When this closing bracket is encountered, any inner blocks that may still be open are closed by default.

$(and $) are used not only to delimit blocks but also to bracket together a sequence of statements to form a *compound statement*. What distinguishes a block from a compound statement is that the former starts with one or more *dynamic declarations*. The purpose of a dynamic declaration is to define a dynamic variable.

1.4 DYNAMIC VARIABLES

Space for a dynamic variable is allocated within the activation record of a block. The variable ceases to exist when control exits from that block. This arrangement has two major advantages. First variables that are temporary by nature need occupy memory space only while they are being processed. Second, the recursive use of an identifier, i.e. a reference to it during its own computation, causes a new instance of it to be created, so that its original value does not become overwritten. We shall have more to say about recursion later when we discuss functions.

Dynamic variables are declared by the keyword LET. Thus we might begin a new block as follows:

```
$(
LET linelength = 62
```

which would introduce a local identifier linelength and set it to an initial (default) right value of 62. In this example, we have initialised the variable to a constant; but there is no reason why a variable could not be used, provided of course that its right value is known at this point. Thus

```
$(
LET x = 62
LET tenex = 10 * x
```

would initialise tenex to 620.

If you do not wish to initialise a local variable, several implementations allow you to declare it thus

```
LET newlocal = ?
```

so that a system-dependent "neutral" value will be assigned initially. Some compilers register an error if the right value of a variable initialised as ? is referred to in the program before a right value can be assigned to it.

It is also possible to define several local names in a single declaration thus

```
LET x, y, z = 0, 25, maxheight
```

There is an alternative form which is known as a *simultaneous declaration*; for example

```
LET x = 0
AND y = 25
AND z = maxheight
```

which is equivalent to it.

The components of a compound or simultaneous decaration are assumed to be executed simultaneously. In practice they are probably executed in sequence as written, so the value of y after

```
LET x, y = 20, x + 30
```

is probably 50, though this cannot be guaranteed. The declaration

    LET x, y = y + 20, 30

will probably assign a neutral value to x, and may even lead to a
run-time error. Compound and simultaneous decarations that are inter-
dependent are best avoided, if only for the sake of portability.

An important limitation in BCPL that does not appear in other
block-structured languages is that dynamic variables are accessible *only*
from the blocks in which they were declared. They are not even accessible from blocks enclosed within these blocks. This limitation, which
arises from the policy of simplification in the design of BCPL, and from
a desire to reduce overheads during execution, can cause some difficulty
to users familiar with Pascal, or even C. The BCPL diagnostic message
"dynamic free variable used" often arises from an attempt to do something that is perfectly legitimate in either of these two languages.

Strictly speaking, declarations are delimited by a semicolon. However, the structure of BCPL is such that the compiler can usually tell where
one declaration ends and another begins. Nevertheless, to aid readability, it is good practice either to insert semicolons or else put declarations
on separate lines.

1.5 STATIC VARIABLES

There are two sorts of variables that are non-local, that is, variables for
which space is reserved throughout the whole execution of the program.
These are known as *static variables* and *globals*. Static variables are
declared and initialised with the keyword STATIC and section brackets,
thus

    STATIC $(maxheight = 155 $)

If several static variables appear in the same declaration, then they are
separated by semicolons

    STATIC $(joe=1; fred=2; willy=74 $)

or, for better readability, newlines.

Static variables have the advantage over dynamic variables that the
former are accessible anywhere within a program module. Thus they
can be used to provide communication between dynamic blocks. Space
is usually allocated for them in the same area of memory as program
code. This means that they cease to be variable if the code is eventually
blown into ROM. Furthermore, BCPL was designed from the outset so

that it can be written as a set of separately compiled modules; and static variables have the disadvantage that they are accessible only within the module in which they are declared. For these two reasons, static variables are less useful than . . .

1.6 GLOBALS

A BCPL program can consist of several separately compiled modules. Global variables are designed to be accessible from all modules making up a single program. The technique whereby BCPL modules communicate is slightly unconventional. Instead of undergoing a separate linking operation to assign left values to externals, a BCPL module makes all its external references through the medium of a *global vector*, which contains all the variables that have been declared to be global, as well as pointers to all global functions and routines. In fact the first 100 or so locations of the global vector contain pointers to all the BCPL library procedures. The main advantage of such an arrangement is that it makes the linking of separately compiled modules extremely fast. The conventional method of linking can take substantially longer than compiling a single module, and can make program development tedious on a slow system.

A global variable declaration, in contrast to a local or static variable declaration, does not initialise the variable. Instead it allocates it a specified position in the global vector. Any globals you create have to be allocated positions above those already reserved for entries to the BCPL library. The first unallocated global location is often passed by the system as a predeclared constant. A typical global declaration might be:

```
GLOBAL $(
            common1 : 100
            common2 : 101
            functabc : 102
            routinxyz : 103
        $)
```

Alternatively the items can be written on a single line, delimited by semicolons.

1.7 CONSTANTS

Manifest constants are names that are permanently associated with particular values. They exist only at compile time, the names being replaced by the corresponding values in the object code. The declaration

> MANIFEST $(height = 256 ; width = 512 $)

declares two manifest constants with the values specified. As with static and global declarations, the semicolons can be replaced for better readability by newlines.

1.8 STRUCTURES

BCPL, being a single-type language, has no built-in structures. However, it is possible in BCPL to reserve a sequence of dynamic locations and treat them thereafter as a vector. The declaration

> LET v = VEC n

allocates the next n+1 cells on the stack. It also reserves a further cell, associates it with the name v, and places in it the address of the first of the vector cells. The dimension n must be a constant expression, i.e. a literal or a manifest name or an expression involving either or both. This is so that the size of the activation record can be determined at compile time. It is a restrictive rule; but it can be to some extent overcome by the use of the function APTOVEC, which we discuss in Chapter 3, or by the use of other functions specific to particular implementations.

If v points to the start of a vector, then the "contents" expression !v evaluates to yield the content of the first cell in the vector (i.e. the "zeroth"). The symbol ! is given dyadic significance in BCPL to enable it to be used to index other items of the vector. Thus vector items after the first can be addressed as v!1, v!2 and so on, v!0 being the same as !v. The last item is v!n; so the vector contains not n but n+1 cells. This confers the advantage (among others) that we can handle a vector of n elements and index them at option from either 0 or 1. But notice that you can "index" any identifier in BCPL, whether or not it has been the subject of a vector declaration.

Because BCPL has only one data type, indexing is always by single word cells. Consequently the left value of v!j, i.e.@v!j, is the same as v + j, which in turn is the same as j + v. Thus we can as well write j!v as v!j. This is not so in C, which is a typed language, and indexes an array in accordance with the size of its base type.

As we have already seen, !v is equivalent to a name, and may therefore be used on the left-hand side of an assignment. The same applies to any subscript vector expression. Thus

```
v!3 := 1234
```

assigns the value 1234 to item 3 (the fourth item) in the vector. The situation after such an assignment might be illustrated thus:

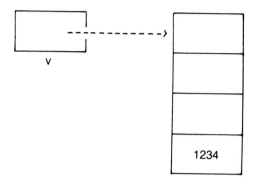

1.9 STRINGS

Strings in BCPL are best thought of as constants. A string is represented by an address pointing to a sequence of bytes in static memory. The first byte contains a count of the number of characters in the string (which limits BCPL strings to a length of 255 bytes); and the remainder contain the characters themselves. The string itself is written between double quotes.

A string may be be given an identifier through a dynamic declaration such as

```
LET message = "press space bar"
```

It is important to understand though that the identifier message is thereby associated not with the string itself but with a pointer to it. Thus

```
x := message
```

places in x a copy of the pointer to the string "press space bar". The statement

```
x := !message
```

places in x the contents of the first word in the string. In a 32-bit BCPL implementation this will probably be the length byte followed by the first three bytes in the string.

Strings are often quoted as constants in the body of a program, as for instance

```
message := "press space bar"
```

or as arguments to suitable routines, for instance

    WRITES("press space bar")

Notice that

    WRITEHEX(!message)
    or WRITEHEX(!"press space bar")

should print

    0F 70 72 65

BCPL strings cannot simply be compared, as they are in BASIC, with comparison operators. The comparison

    "A" = "A"

in BCPL is false because the two As occupy different memory locations, and therefore have different pointers. String comparison must therefore use special functions, which many implementations provide.

The symbol * is used as an escape character to enable "hidden" characters to be included in strings. Thus *N denotes newline, *T tab, *P newpage, *B backspace and *S space. Some systems include also *Xnn, where nn represents two hexadecimal digits, to permit any other non-print code in the repertoire to be included. The asterisk is also used to escape the special significance of ' and ". These are included in strings as *' and *" respectively. A single asterisk should appear in a string as **.

The same escaped symbols can be used too in defining characters. Thus '*N' is a single byte, which probably has the value 13. '**' probably has decimal value 42 and so on. It is important to appreciate the difference between characters and strings of one letter. The right value of 'a' is a word cell containing the number 97 (decimal) at its right-hand end, while that of "a" is a pointer to a byte containing the number 1, which is followed by one containing 97.

1.10 FUNCTIONS

A function is a named expression. In BCPL a function name is distinguished from that of a variable by the use of a pair of parentheses. Thus in the simplest case a function is declared by a statement of the form

    LET fname() = expression

The value to be associated with fname() is the value obtained by evaluating the expression at the time that fname() is *called*, i.e. quoted after being defined, as for instance in

```
x := fname()
```

It is evident that the expression appearing on the right-hand side of a function declaration can contain only constants and variables visible at that point. But a function constitutes a block; and in BCPL there is no access from a block to dynamic variables declared in other blocks. This means that the expression in the simple function example we have just given can use only static and global variables. This would be most restrictive, were it not for the fact, first, that we can declare variables local to a function, and we can pass copies of dynamic variables to it as *arguments* or *parameters*.

Identifiers appearing between the parentheses after a function name are treated as *dummy arguments*, which may legitimately be used in the expression. Thus for instance we might write

```
LET sumsq(x, y) = x*x + y*y
```

where the operators * and + have the usual significance of multiplication and addition. When the function sumsq is called, real parameters, which must be visible at the point of call, are substituted for the dummy arguments wherever they appear in the function definition. Thus the following sequence:

```
LET p = 3
AND q = 4
AND r = ?
AND sumsq(x, y) = x*x + y*y
r := sumsq(p, q)
```

should result in 25 being assigned to r.

If expressions were confined to those conventionally found in other languages, then functions in BCPL would be very restricted indeed, rather like statement functions in FORTRAN. But BCPL provides an operator VALOF, which enables a function to be defined in terms of a sequence of commands. VALOF must be matched with a RESULTIS command within the block. For instance

```
LET gcd(a, b) = VALOF
$(
    $(
        IF a > b THEN a := a−b
        IF a < b THEN b := b−a
        IF a = b THEN RESULTIS a
    $) REPEAT
$)
```

The effect of RESULTIS is to escape from the REPEAT loop and return to the calling expression, with the value of a substituted for the function name in the original call.

Once a function has been defined as an explicit block between section brackets, the way is open to provide it with dynamic variables of its own. These of course are visible only within the function itself; but they are useful for holding temporary values while the function is being evaluated. We shall not give an example here. Plenty of instances can be found among the examples in Chapter 4.

Parameters in BCPL are passed *by value*. What this means is that new (dynamic) cells are created on the stack to receive *copies* of the real parameters when the call is made. Thus, if we write

    gcd(1443, 1885)

then 1443 is assigned to the argument a and 1885 is assigned to b. a and b are lost on exit from the function; but the RESULTIS ensures that a *copy* of the last value of a is passed back.

Normally call by value means that parameters cannot be altered as a side-effect of the function call. However, certain objects, such as vectors and strings, are defined as pointers; and it is then quite possible for the function to have a side-effect upon them. Of course if you wish you can deliberately provoke a side-effect on any operand by passing the address instead of the value. The parameter is then said to be passed *by reference*. An example of this technique appears in the next section but one.

1.11 RECURSION

Functions in BCPL are always *recursive*. In the simplest case this means that a function name is visible within its own definition. For instance a factorial can be computed in BCPL with a function of the form

    LET fact(n) = n=0 → 1, n*fact(n−1)

The significance of the operators → and , is that if the condition n=0 is true then 1 is returned as the value of the function: if not, then the product n*fact(n−1) is computed. This latter leads to the creation of another activation record associated with the function fact, the value of the argument being one less than it was in the previous activation record. In fact in all n activation records will be created before the value of the argument is reduced to zero. Of course this is not a very good way to compute a factorial since, despite the simplifications inherent in BCPL, each successive call imposes overheads in time and memory requirements. Nevertheless, a recursively defined function is often easier to understand, and hence to debug, than one based on a looping algorithm. Deep recursion can cause a program to run out of stack space. So programs with a lot of recursion often have to be rerun after requesting more workspace from the operating system.

Apart from itself, a function declared by LET can only refer to function names appearing earlier in the text. However, it is possible to declare several functions simultaneously by using the word AND, thus

```
LET f1() = ....

AND f2() = ....

AND f3() = ....
```

The effect is to permit forward reference as well as backward, and hence allow mutual recursion between functions in the same declaration. We deal more fully with this later when we discuss scope and visibility.

1.12   ROUTINES

A routine is a complete statement in itself, and therefore does not return a value. Its declaration is similar to that of a function, except that the word BE is substituted for the = thus

```
LET rname(arguments) BE block
```

Routines are called as commands, real parameters appearing between the parentheses. As with functions, the parentheses must appear even if there are no arguments.

To illustrate the idea of passing parameters by reference, we shall repeat the gcd function given above but write it as a routine, with the result being passed back by a side-effect on the second parameter.

```
LET rgcd(a, pointb) BE
    $(
        $(
            IF a > !pointb THEN a := a − !pointb
            IF a < !pointb THEN !pointb := !pointb − a
            IF a = !pointb THEN RETURN
        $) REPEAT
    $)
```

This routine should be invoked by a statement of the form

    rgcd(x, @y)

when the value of y will be altered by the routine to become the value of the gcd.

    Admittedly this example is a bit artificial. A function is the natural structure for computing a gcd. However, at best a function can return only one value. If more than one is to be returned then side effects have to be used. One way of making a function return several values is to put them in a vector and pass a single pointer to it. Remember that the vector must have been declared *outside* the function, for anything local disappears on exit.

    It is sometimes a good idea to declare a function when a routine might appear superficially to be more appropriate. For instance when we issue a command to a peripheral device we usually want to know whether or not it has "worked". We can get this information by designing the command as a function that returns either TRUE or FALSE according as the command has or has not been accepted. Indeed such a command could be designed to return different codes for different error conditions.

1.13 SCOPE AND VISIBILITY

The term *scope* unhappily has been used in two senses in computing. One is to denote the part of a program over which an identifier may legitimately be used: the other is to denote the extent of time during which storage is allocated for it. These two are not always the same; so to avoid confusion we shall use the term *visibility* to denote the first meaning and *lifespan* to denote the second. With block-structured languages such as BCPL, visibility is limited so that the same name may be used differently in different parts of the program.

    The visibility and lifetime of a global identifier is every module in which that identifier is declared GLOBAL. The lifetime of a static identifier is the same; but the visibility of a static identifier declared at the top level, i.e. outside a function or routine block, is the remainder of that module. If a static declaration is made within a block, then its visibility is the remainder of the block. Notice that static cells remain allocated throughout a program even though parts of the program may be outside their visibility. The lifetime of a dynamic name is the remainder of the block in which it was declared; but its visibility in BCPL, in common with other block-structured languages, does not extend to the bodies of functions or routines called from within the block.

Function and routine names declared at the top level can be either static or global. If the name has already appeared in a global declaration, then that global cell receives a pointer to the start of the code. If not, then a static cell is created to hold the pointer. In this case the visibility extends from the declaration to the end of the module, except that, in the case of simultaneous declarations, the whole of the simultaneous declaration is included.

Because libraries are separate modules, library routines have to be declared global in any modules where they are used. Libraries can be declared *in toto* by incorporating a header. A header, or any other file for that matter, can be incorporated in a piece of source text by means of the directive GET. For instance, global declarations for the standard library, as well as a few manifest declarations, are contained in a file LIBHDR that is provided with the compiler. Thus

```
GET "LIBHDR"
```

on a line by itself would ensure that the module has access to all the library functions and routines. A file incorporated by GET may itself contain GET directives; so you can augment the standard library with one of your own.

A function or routine declared within a block is local to that block unless its name has previously been declared global, and there has been no use of the same name at a higher level. We must also consider the visibility of dynamic variables in blocks containing function or routine declarations. In most block-structured languages dynamic variables include in their scope any inner block within the same outer block. This rule applies in BCPL to simple blocks constructed with section brackets, but not to function or routine blocks. Thus in the structure

```
LET F(x) = VALOF
$(
        LET y = 0
        AND G(t) = VALOF
        $(
                ...... // region 1
        $)
        ...... // region 2
$)
```

the argument x and the variable y are visible anywhere in region 2 but nowhere in region 1. It follows that, if either is to be used with function

G, then either it, or a pointer to it, must be passed explicitly as an argument of G. The reason for this rule is to keep the BCPL run-time system simple. A BCPL function or routine "knows" nothing of the dynamic environment within which it was declared or called. It can operate only on its own activation record (which of course includes the arguments), augmented by whatever it can reach statically or through the global vector.

Because of the BCPL limitation on the visibility of dynamic variables, the fact that vectors can only be allocated dynamically takes a little getting used to. One can create static vectors of constants with the operator TABLE (see the next chapter); but variable vectors must be declared with VEC, so they are local and cannot be used in other routines. A partial solution is to create a *static* pointer to a dynamic vector: for instance

```
STATIC $( list = 0 $)

LET listproc() BE
$(
        LET V = VEC listlength
        list := V
        . . . . . . . .
```

But this arrangement abounds with pitfalls. Remember that the vector is still dynamic, and will get overwritten as soon as control comes out of the routine listproc and creates a new record on the stack. list, though static, can legitimately be used therefore only by routines called from within listproc.

Another possible solution is to declare the vector at the highest possible level, and pass the pointer to it as a parameter, thus

```
LET list = VEC listlength
AND listproc(v) BE
$(
. . . . .
$)


. . . . .


listproc(vec)
```

1.14 PROGRAMS

A BCPL program is a set of one or more separately compiled modules, each consisting of a sequence of declarations. These will include MAN-IFEST and GLOBAL, and possibly STATIC declarations, followed by one or more function and routine declarations. One of the latter must be a routine called START(), the beginning of which is the entry point for the program as a whole. START() is a global. In fact it is usually GLOBAL!1.

Chapter 2

BCPL Expressions and Commands

Expressions are sequences of operators and *primaries*. In BCPL there are FOUR sorts of primaries: quoted constants, identifiers, function calls, and expressions in parentheses. The effect on an expression of enclosing part of it in parentheses is the usual one of forcing that part to be evaluated ahead of the rest. The simplest expression is of course a single primary; and the value of such an expression is the right value of the primary.

The manner in which an expression is evaluated depends upon the *precedence* or *binding power* of its operators. Thus the expression

$3 + 5 * 2$

yields the value 13 not 16 because the operator * has a greater binding power than + . Where operators have the same binding power, they are elaborated from left to right.

Because earlier versions of BCPL were implemented on machines with a restricted (6-bit) character set, a number of synonyms exists for individual operators. These have been preserved in later implementations to give some portability to existing BCPL programs.

2.1 ARITHMETIC OPERATORS

Arithmetic operators are classed as multiplying operators and adding operators. The adding operators are + and −. The use of − can give rise to negative numbers, whose representation is machine-dependent, though most machines today use twos complement. Both + and − may be used monadically. The value of +x is x, and that of −x is the same as 0 − x. The treatment of overflow is undefined.

Multiplying operators have a greater binding power than adding operators. They are * (multiply), / (divide), and REM (find remainder). Division gives an integer result. If the operands are both positive this involves truncation, so

$x − x$ REM y is the same as $x / y * y$

If either is, or both are, negative, then the result is not defined, though the relation just given may still apply.

2.2 RELATIONS

The most commonly found relational operators are >, <, =, >=, <= and
NE. The following synonyms are found for the first five: GR, LS, EQ, GE,
LE . The symbol ~=, where ~ may be replaced by some other symbol
for "not", is also found as a synonym for NE. Notice that <> cannot be
used to denote inequality. Some implementations use this to provide a
shorthand form of compound command, binding two commands
together without the need for section brackets.

Relations have a lower binding power than arithmetic operators, so
that

    a + b > x − y

does what would naturally be expected, viz. yields a truth value by
comparing the values of the two arithmetic expressions.

2.3 SHIFT OPERATORS

BCPL allows for efficient bit manipulation by providing left and right
shift operators, << and >>. LSHIFT and RSHIFT are found as synonyms.
They return the bit-pattern of the first operand shifted by the number of
places given as the second operand. The vacant places in either sense of
shift are filled with zeros, and bits shifted off are lost. The effect is the
same as multiplication or unsigned integer division by a power of two.
Thus

    12 << 3 yields 96
and   26 >> 2 yields 6

The shift operators have a lower binding power than relations to the
left of them, and a higher binding power than relations to the right.
Thus

    x >> 2 < x / 4

yields the value FALSE while

    x / 4 < x >> 2

yields the machine representation of TRUE (typically a full word of
ones) shifted to the right two places.

2.4 LOGICAL OPERATORS

The logical operators have a strict precedence among themselves. The highest is the monadic NOT or ~, which inverts each bit in the operand. Next comes the conjunction operator & with its synonyms /\ and LOGAND, followed by disjunction, |.\/ or LOGOR. Two further logical operators are provided. These are EQV and NEQV the latter being the exclusive OR operator, and the former its inverse. These four dyadic operators are all commutative; and their effects can be illustrated by the following table.

		&	|	EQV	NEQV
0	0	0	0	1	0
0	1	0	1	0	1
1	1	1	1	1	0

Other logical operators can be constructed from the basic five. For instance implication is

NOT a | b

and NAND is either

NOT(a & b)   or   NOT a | NOT b

The logical operators all have lower precedence than the relations. The expression a<b & b<c does what is expected; i.e. it is true if b lies between a and c. But BCPL allows an extended form of relation; so the same condition can be expressed as a<b<c. We can, for instance, determine if an ASCII character c is alphabetic with the expression

64 < c < 91 | 96 < c < 123

parentheses being unnecessary. Relational expressions can be extended to an arbitrary length, for instance

a > b < c = d

which has the obvious interpretation

a > b & b > c & c = d

The logical operators are elaborated in the context of operands that are either truth values or binary strings. This means that the representations for TRUE and FALSE are chosen to avoid contradiction. Typically FALSE is all zeros and TRUE all ones, though any nonzero word is taken as true in any context in which it is interpreted as a condition.

2.5 CONDITIONAL EXPRESSIONS

As well as conditional statements (which we shall deal with later), BCPL provides a conditional form of expression, which properly used can lead to economies both in code and in object programs. The expression

  a → b, c

where a, b and c may themselves be expressions, is evaluated as follows: a is first elaborated to yield a truth value. If this is true, then b is elaborated to yield the value of the expression: if it is false, then b is ignored and the value of the expression is that of c. Thus we read the expression as "if a then b otherwise c.

The operator → has a lower precedence than any of the logical operators. This ensures that a is fully evaluated before its truth value is tested. However, to save execution time, implementors generally arrange that b and c are not evaluated until after → has been applied, and moreover that only one of the two is actually evaluated. This can lead to unexpected results if side-effects are involved. When two or more conditions appear in the same expression, the operators associate to the right. Thus

  a → b, c → d, e

is equivalent to

  a → b, (c → d, e)

The expression in brackets is not evaluated at all if a is true.

2.6 ADDRESSING OPERATORS

We introduced the addressing operators in the previous chapter. They come right at the top of the priority table. @, and ! in its monadic role, have the same binding power, which is below that of ! in its dyadic role. This means that

  !v!2

is evaluated by treating word 2 of vector v as a pointer, and taking the right value of the cell indicated, thus:

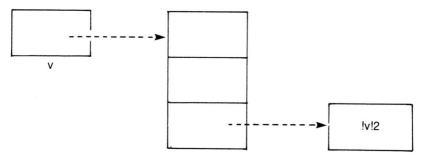

This is not what left-to-right association might imply, which is:

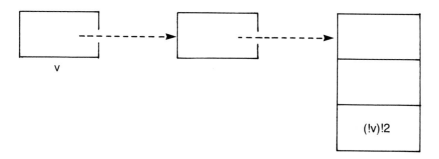

2.7   TABLE and VALOF

Two further operators remain; and these have the lowest binding value of all. The operator TABLE is used to create a static array of constants. Thus the expression

      TABLE 2, 3, 5, 7, 9, 11

creates a sequence of six static cells. The value of the expression is a pointer to the first of these; so, for example,

      3!TABLE 2, 3, 5, 7, 9, 11

has the value 7. If you wish, you can assign a table pointer to a variable, thus

      primes := TABLE 2, 3, 5, 7, 9, 11

so that the table is accessible wherever primes is visible. Tables are constructed at compile time; so the operator TABLE must be followed by a sequence of *constant* expressions, i.e. expressions that can be evaluated at compile time. You cannot, for instance, construct a table of addresses by this method.

VALOF we have already met in connection with function definition. It is a monadic operator that is used to convert a command into an expression. Since a command does not normally return a value, it must be forced to do so by including at least one RESULTIS command, which means that it should usually be a compound command or a block. The value of the VALOF expression is the value returned by the first RESULTIS encountered. Although the primary use of VALOF is in declaring functions, it is often used in a larger expression or as the right-hand side of an assignment. For instance, one might look up a vector to find, say, the first zero, thus

```
zpos := VALOF
        FOR n = 0 TO vlength DO IF v!n = 0 THEN RESULTIS n
```

In summary then we may set out the BCPL operators in order of precedence thus:

operators	synonyms
function call	
! (dyadic)	
@ ! (monadic)	
∗ / REM	
+ −	
> < = >= <= NE << >>	GT LT EQ GE LE ~= LSHIFT RSHIFT
NOT	~
&	/\ LOGAND
|	\/ LOGOR
EQV NEQV	
→	
TABLE	
VALOF	

2.8 COMMANDS

Nominally commands are separated by semicolons or newlines. But the BCPL compiler can generally tell when one command ends and another begins; so the semicolon is seldom necessary. Nevertheless the full rules for determining when a command separator is absolutely necessary are quite complicated, so it is advisable either to insert the semicolon or to start every new command on a new line. This leaves just one ambiguity. If an expression or command happens to extend over more than one line, the compiler might take the first part of it, up to the newline, as the whole. This can be avoided by ensuring that the expression is incomplete at the line end, either by making the last symbol an unresolved dyadic operator, or by enclosing the whole expression in parentheses. Incidentally, BCPL does not have a null statement. A construction such as

```
FOR j=1 TO 5 DO
```

will repeat the statement that starts on the next line. If you really want a "do nothing" loop, you must do something trivial instead, such as assigning an identifier to itself.

Commands can be simple or compound. A compound command is a sequence of commands enclosed between section brackets. A block is similar to a compound command, except that a block starts with one or more declarations, and thereby modifies the visible scope of dynamic variables. Both blocks and commands count syntactically as single commands. Because control structures in BCPL are open-ended: for instance, the "if" structure is not terminated by a semicolon or a matching "fi" as it is in other programming languages, we need compound commands to indicate the limits of a conditional command or the body of a loop.

Commands can be labelled, a label being any legal identifier followed by a colon. Labels are generally used in connection with the GOTO statement. You will probably have been taught that the use of GOTO is the next thing to a sin against the Holy Ghost; and indeed there are enough structured commands in most languages, particularly in BCPL, to make the use of GOTO strictly unnecessary. However, there are occasions when the use of GOTO can lead to more compact code than the use of a better structured command, for instance

```
GOTO x > y → here, there
```

and compactness can sometimes be an overriding consideration.

Labels in BCPL are handled in the same way as function and routine names; and you can enter a routine simply by "going to" its name. A problem will then probably arise on exit, when the system will try to remove an activation record. Nevertheless it will sometimes be possible to generate a faster piece of code by entering one routine in the conventional way, going to another routine, and exiting conventionally from that.

The value associated with a label is the address of the first instruction in the compiled command that follows it. In other words, a label simply names a static cell. Consequently in BCPL, in contrast to other languages, including C, labels can be manipulated like other identifiers; but such manipulation, while doubtless very clever, can often lead to more problems than it solves.

2.9 ASSIGNMENTS

We have already given examples of assignments in BCPL. A single assignment can involve several left-right pairs; for instance

    n, x, ptr := 12, y−z, @joe

The assignments are made in strict correspondence: n becomes 12, x becomes (y−z), and so on. Values are assigned in sequence. Thus

    a, b := b, a

does not exchange the values of a and b; but assigns the same value (probably b) to both. The order of assignment is undefined. Though it will generally be found to be from left to right, it is not safe to assume that this will always be so if you want your programs to be portable. The use of multiple assignments can simplify program text by avoiding the need for compound commands in certain cases.

2.10 ROUTINES

Routine calls of course are instances of commands. In a call of the form

    routn(p1, p2, p3, . . . pn)

the parameters can be any form of expression. They are evaluated to right values, which are then copied into new cells in the activation record of the routine. These replace the dummy arguments when the routine is elaborated. BCPL has the unusual feature, however, that the number of parameters passed may be less than the number of arguments defined. Parameters are matched with arguments in sequence starting with the first; and arguments unmatched are left undefined.

A routine returns no value. Commands are executed until either the end of the block is reached or a RETURN is encountered, when control is passed back to the command following the call, and the activation record of the block is removed. Another command that can cause exit from a block is FINISH. This returns control to the operating system or monitor, and deletes the whole working stack. In short, it terminates the program.

2.11 CONDITIONAL COMMANDS

In a command of the form

    IF t THEN c

t is an expression that is evaluated to yield a truth value, and c is a command that may or may not be compound. c is executed if the value of t represents true, not otherwise. A synonym of THEN is DO. THEN (or DO) may be omitted if it is followed immediately by another keyword. Thus you can write for instance

    IF t GOTO lab1

A second conditional command

    UNLESS t THEN c

gives the possibility of execution when t is false. Neither IF nor UNLESS admits an ELSE option. This is provided by a separate construction of the form

    TEST t THEN c1 ELSE c2

OR is a synonym for ELSE.

2.12 REPETITION

A statement can be repeated an indefinite number of times by following it with the keyword REPEAT. In an industrial control application, the whole of a program might be a single REPEAT loop intended to be executed for ever, or at least until the equipment breaks down. In general, however, some form of exit from the loop will be needed. If the loop appears in a function or routine, this can be achieved with a RESULTIS or RETURN statement, or even a FINISH. If not, or if you do not want to return to the call, then you can use a BREAK statement, which causes control to be transferred to the statement following the REPEAT.

REPEAT is all that is needed in fact to build any sort of repetitive construction. However, to make programs more readily understood, it is desirable for the terminating condition to be tested at either the beginning or the end of the loop. Moreover, a REPEAT loop is always obeyed at least once unless it was preceded by an IF or UNLESS command to test the condition in advance. BCPL therefore provides four other repetitive commands:

```
c REPEATWHILE t
c REPEATUNTIL t
WHILE t DO c
UNTIL t DO c
```

In the first two of these, c is executed at least once; but in the second two it need not be executed at all. The first and third continue to execute so long as t is true: the second and fourth so long as it is false. Thus

```
c REPEATWHILE t
```

is equivalent to

```
c WHILE t DO c
```

or

```
$( c IF t BREAK $) REPEAT
```

REPEAT, REPEATWHILE and REPEATUNTIL control the shortest possible command. Thus

```
IF t THEN c REPEAT
```

is equivalent to

```
IF t THEN $( c REPEAT $)
```

and

```
x := VALOF c REPEAT
```

is equivalent to

```
x := VALOF $( c REPEAT $)
```

If in doubt, insert the section brackets.

A common requirement is for a "half" loop, in which only part of the loop is obeyed under certain circumstances. In many languages it is necessary to use an "if" and a "goto" to achieve this. In BCPL, if the "half" comes on the last repetition, then a premature exit can be forced by RETURN, RESULTIS or BREAK. However, this does not help if you want to omit part of the loop during a cycle earlier than the last. BCPL therefore provides the command LOOP. This causes the remainder of the controlled statement to be omitted, and repetition to be resumed (if further repetition is called for) at its start. LOOP and BREAK are generally controlled by IF or TEST; and tend to be neater than using GOTO.

2.13   COUNTING LOOPS

A loop can be executed a preset number of times by using a construction of the form

```
FOR n = e1 TO e2 BY k DO c
```

This may be defined in terms of an indefinite loop thus

```
$(
    LET n, f = e1, e2
    UNTIL n > f DO
        $(
            c
            n := n + k
        $)
$)
```

which means that if e1 is greater than e2 the command c does not get executed at all. The loop variable (n in this case) is automatically declared, and it is local to the controlled command. This neatly side-steps the problem, found in other languages, of deciding what its value should be on exit. In BCPL it ceases to exist.

There is a restriction that the loop step k must be a constant expression. One reason for this is so that its sign can be known at compile time. If it is negative, then the expression n > f in the definition given above is replaced by n < f. If the value of k is unity, then both it and the keyword BY preceding it may be omitted. A FOR loop can be left prematurely by RETURN, RESULTIS or BREAK; or part of it may be skipped with a LOOP command. Thus the following block reads characters one by one into a buffer, stopping when either the buffer is full or a newline is read:

```
$(
    LET buf = VEC 127
    FOR i = 0 TO 127 DO
        $(
            char := RDCH()
            IF char = '*N' BREAK
            buf!i := char
        $)
$)
```

2.14 SWITCHES

The construction

```
SWITCHON e INTO cc
```

where cc is a compound command, allows the construction of a switch. Some statements in the compound command must be labelled with either CASE k: where k is a constant expression, or DEFAULT: . At most one statement may carry the default label. The effect of a switch command is to cause expression e to be evaluated. If the result matches any of the cases, then control is transferred to the command so labelled. If not, and there is a default label, then control is transferred to that. Otherwise the whole compound command is ignored, and control is transferred to the command after it.

Under normal circumstances the programmer will wish to execute only the few commands from the selected label up to the next label. The command ENDCASE transfers control direct to the end of the compound statement in much the same way that BREAK transfers control out of a loop. The following example reads text and puts it out again in identical form except that tabs and multiple spaces are replaced with single spaces:

```
$(
    char := RDCH()
    SWITCHON char INTO
        $(
            CASE '*N': NEWLINE(); tag := FALSE
```

```
            ENDCASE
            CASE '*T': CASE '*S': tag := TRUE; LOOP
            CASE endfile: BREAK
            DEFAULT: IF tag THEN WRCH('*S')
            tag := FALSE
        $)
    WRCH(char)
$) REPEAT
```

tag having been declared with the initial value FALSE.

Chapter 3

The BCPL Library

BCPL has no design authority other than the latest book from its designer (see Introduction, reference 9) although there is a user group that publishes its own standard. This means that, while the main part of the language has been largely standardised by usage the library tends to be implementation-dependent. Although several routine and function names are common to all implementations, there are subtle, and sometimes not so subtle, differences in the way they work. We give them here, together with a general description of what they do. This should be taken in conjunction with details supplied by the implementor; and perhaps you should do a bit of experimentation as well.

3.1 INPUT AND OUTPUT STREAMS

The need to provide facilities suitable for all kinds of input and output device is a common problem for designers of programming languages. The solution adopted in BCPL is to use the abstraction of a *data stream*. A stream is a sequence of character codes, some displayable others used only for control, that can be accepted from, or transmitted to, the outside world.

Input and output streams are opened respectively by the functions

```
stream := FINDINPUT("string")
stream := FINDOUTPUT("string")
```

where string is a system-dependent file or device name that may include codes to denote the mode of opening. The functions return an integer stream identifier, or *handle*, which is to be used in the future when referring to that channel. If for any reason the channel cannot be opened, then the functions return zero.

BCPL allows an indefinite number of streams to be open simultaneously, though there will always be a system limit. Only one input and one output stream however can be in use at any one time. They are selected from among those that are currently open by

```
SELECTINPUT(stream)
SELECTOUTPUT(stream)
```

These may be either routines or functions, depending on the implementation. If they are functions, then they return the stream number if
valid, zero if not. Some systems will open and select a standard input
(SYSIN) and a standard output (SYSOUT) stream automatically when
a program starts to execute: others oblige you to do this for yourself.

The read and write routines and functions operate on whatever input
and output streams happen to be selected at the time. The functions
(routines)

```
ENDREAD()
ENDWRITE()
```

close the currently selected input and output streams respectively. If
they are implemented as functions, then they return system-dependent
codes in case of error. The activity involved in closing a stream varies
according to the device involved. Closing a tape file may cause rewind-
ing: closing a file on disc does little more than release the buffer space.

3.2   READING

The fundamental read operation is performed by the function

```
c := RDCH()
```

which assigns to variable c the internal (probably ASCII) value of the
next character in sequence in the currently selected input stream, and
moves the buffer pointer on to the next character in the sequence. On
coming to the end of a file RDCH() returns a value defined by a manifest
declaration as ENDSTREAMCH. Some systems provide a function
UNRDCH() as well. This pushes back the last character read on to the
current input stream, and returns an error value (typically zero) if this
cannot be done, for instance if the stream has only just been opened.

In fact the primitive RDCH() is all that is strictly necessary to read all
sorts of data; but most implementations provide more complex read
functions as well. The commonest is

```
n := READN()
```

which reads a sequence of digits (optionally preceded by a minus) from
the input stream, converts them in decimal radix, and assigns the result
to n. The digits should be terminated by white-space (which includes
newline and tab).

Some systems provide additional read functions to get complete lines
or records from the input stream. In such cases a vector has to be

declared for use as a buffer (in addition to any buffer automatically created by SELECTINPUT) and passed as a parameter. An integer has also to be passed giving the buffer length.

3.3 WRITING

The basic write routine is

WRCH(c)

which places the low-order byte of the right value of c in the next position in the currently selected output stream. In symmetry with READN() there is normally a WRITEN(n), which converts the right value of n into decimal and outputs it in a field of whatever width is needed. To assist in tabulating results, most systems offer several other output routines, such as WRITEHEX(n, w), WRITEOCT(n, w) and WRITED(n, w), which output n as a hexadecimal, octal or decimal number right justified in a field of width w. If the parameter w is omitted, a default width will be used.

There is normally a routine

WRITES(string)

for writing strings. The string can be a simple character string; or it can contain the following formatting symbols:

*N	newline
*S	space
*T	tab
**	*
*'	'
*"	"

possibly among others.

More useful still is the general formatted output routine

WRITEF(format, a, b, ...)

This outputs a, b, etc. according to instructions embedded in the format string. Each instruction is preceded by a % symbol. The following is a typical minimum set:

%N	decimal number
%S	string
%C	character
%O	octal
%X	hexadecimal

Thus for instance the formatted write call

WRITEF("name %S status *"%C*" age %N*N", name, marital, age)

might produce the output

name James Jones status "m" age 45

A percent can be included in a format string as %%.

3.4 PACKED STRINGS

For the sake of compactness, strings are normally handled in packed form, four characters to a word. However, they cannot conveniently be processed in this form, so BCPL provides routines to unpack them, one character to a word, and to pack them again.

UNPACKSTRING(string, v)

puts the characters of string one by one into the low-order end of v!1, v!2 etc., with the number of characters in the string stored in v!0. Conversely

PACKSTRING(v, string)

packs v!0 characters from the low end of v!1 etc. into string. The definition of WRITEF (see below) is a good illustration of the way to handle strings in BCPL.

Many systems provide an alternative contents operator to !, which permits bytes to be addressed direct. Typically the operator is %.

Thus s%n would refer to the nth *byte* in the string s, in contrast to s!n, which denotes the nth (4-byte) word. If we

LET s = "seperate"

then we can correct the spelling by writing

s%4 := 'a'

This facility is most likely to be found on byte-addressed machines, of which microprocessors are today the commonest examples. Actual pointer values of course depend on the implementation; but we may imagine that on such systems, the address associated with s!n is 4*(s+n). If, as is likely, the system constrains strings to start on word boundaries, then the address associated with s%n by the same token is 4*s+n. Consequently, while s!n is the same as n!s, the expressions s%n and n%s can have very different values. The value of s%n is undefined, and could lead to an error trap.

Routine WRITE F.

```
LET WRITEF(s, a, b, c, d, e, f, g, h) BE
    $(
        LET v = VEC 256
        LET param, j = @s, 1
        UNPACKSTRING(s, v)
        FOR i=1 TO v!0
        $(
            LET c = v!i
            TEST c = '%'
            THEN
                $(
                    LET val = param!j
                    i, j := i+1, j+1
                    SWITCHON v!i INTO
                    $(
                        CASE 'C': WRITEC(val); ENDCASE
                        CASE 'S': WRITES(val); ENDCASE
                        CASE 'N': WRITEN(val); ENDCASE
                        CASE 'O': WRITEOCT(val); ENDCASE
                        CASE 'H': WRITEHEX(val); ENDCASE
                        DEFAULT: j := j-1; WRITEC(v!i)
                    $)
                $)
            OR  WRITEC(c)
        $)
    $)
```

Other versions of BCPL, generally those implemented on word-addressed machines, provide the same facilities less neatly with the aid of a function

```
b := GETBYTE(word, offset)
```

and a routine

```
PUTBYTE(word, offset, b)
```

word here is a word address, and offset a value in the range 0 .. 3. These functions may appear on byte-addressed machines for compatibility.

3.5 DYNAMIC MEMORY

It will be remembered that the lengths of vectors in BCPL must be known at compile time. This rule leads to valuable simplifications both in the compiler and in the semantics of the language; but it can be rather restrictive, particularly in the context of array processing. In partial alleviation of this situation, BCPL provides a function

APTOVEC(f, n)

which returns the result of applying function f to a newly created vector of (variable) length n. A (syntactically illegal) definition of APTOVEC might be

```
LET APTOVEC(f, n) = VALOF
            $(
                LET v = VEC n
                RESULTIS f(v, n)
            $)
```

The other difficulty with vectors in BCPL is that they are allocated dynamically on the stack, and cease to exist when control exits from the routine in which they were declared. This makes it difficult to structure vector-handling programs as separate modules. However, fortunately, most modern operating systems have an area of free memory, called a *heap*, from which additional space can be claimed during execution. Implementations on such systems provide a function of the form

v := GETVEC(n)

which returns a pointer to a vector of n+1 words in free memory.

GETVEC will normally have an obverse such as FREEVEC(v) to return surplus space to the garbage collector: something that the "tidy" programmer will want to make proper use of. The primary intention of heap storage allocation is to enable programs to adjust memory in accordance with needs during various stages of execution. The lifetime of a GETVEC vector extends up to the corresponding FREEVEC call, and its visibility is that of its pointer; so the facility can be used too in BCPL to provide what are essentially static vectors. An instance of this use appears in example 4 in the next chapter. Systems that permit working space to be allocated dynamically from a *heap* have no need of the APTOVEC function, though it may still be provided for the sake of compatibility.

3.6   STARTING AND STOPPING

The BCPL user must supply one routine called START(). Control is transferred to the entry point of this routine when the program is loaded. START() is then executed up to its final command, or until a RETURN statement transfers control back to the operating system. To terminate execution at any point in any other routine and return to the operating system the command FINISH is used. Most implementations also provide a routine STOP(n), which not only finishes but also returns a code n to indicate the reason for termination.

Diagnostic information can be obtained through a routine ABORT(n), which provides a backtrack of routine and function calls leading up to its call. A good implementation will incorporate ABORT calls in several library functions and routines to assist with debugging. ABORT generally makes use of two other routines that are sometimes provided as globals too. These are BACKTRACE and MAPSTORE. The former lists the functions and routines leading to the call in reverse order, together with a print-out of the top few levels of the stack on each call. MAPSTORE gives the global vector and the locations of all routines and functions.

3.7   RUN-TIME STRUCTURE OF BCPL

Every programming language defines a notional object machine. That defined by BCPL, like that of any block-structured language, has a stack for its working memory. On every entry to a new block a new activation record is created on the stack. The structure of such an object record is

R	L	args	locals	working space

R is the return link, indicating the point in the code to which control is to return on exit from the current block. L points to the start of the previous activation record, which will become the top record when the current record is deleted. Because BCPL function and routine blocks punch a hole in the visible scope of variables called in outer blocks, there is no need for a static link to provide access to the latter.

If a stack record was created through a call with arguments, then these come next on the stack; though, if the machine has enough fast registers, the arguments and the quantities referred to above as R and L may be duplicated in, or replaced by, these. Above the arguments on the stack come the local variables, which will have been created by LET or AND commands at the start of the block. Above these is the working space for the block, where temporary values created by the code will be put during the computation. Notice that the lengths of vectors must be constant expressions; so the amount of stack needed is well defined every time a block is entered. In the case of functions, in contrast to routines, the record is preceded on the stack by an uninitialised location intended to hold the value returned by the function.

In contrast to most block-structured languages, BCPL permits a direct jump from an inner block to an outer block containing it, i.e. from a higher to a lower level on the stack. Such a jump is performed typically in the case of exceptions — events that occur during execution as a result of unusual conditions in the data. These sometimes, but not always, arise from errors or unusual conditions on peripheral machines. By providing a direct jump out of a block, rather than obliging control to retrace the full sequence of calls that got it there, BCPL can save code in object programs. A jump out of a block involves two things: going to a label in another block, and restoring the stack to a level appropriate for the code following that label. The jump is performed by using the routine

    LONGJUMP(level, label)

The destination label must have been declared globally. The level parameter is implementation-dependent. It can only be obtained by a call to the function LEVEL(), which must have been performed earlier while control was in the routine containing the jump label. The level can be passed to the function containing the long jump either as a parameter or as a global.

3.8 FLOATING POINT

Although BCPL does not incorporate a real-number type, many programs do call for floating-point quantities. Indeed it is practically impossible to perform screen graphics without them. Consequently most implementors provide floating point in some form, and do it in a manner that depends on the floating-point representation in the host machine. If floating-point numbers can be represented by data units the same length as a BCPL word, then all that is necessary is to provide a second set of arithmetic operators to handle words in floating-point format. There is also a requirement for FIX and FLOAT operators for conversion, and facilities for input and output in floating-point format.

On machines where floating-point numbers are double-precision, they must be represented in BCPL by a vector of length 2. There must then be a set of "vector" functions FADD, FSUB, FDIV and so on to perform elementary arithmetic. There may also be functions (or a single composite function) to perform trigonometrical and exponential evaluation.

3.9 ASSEMBLER CODE

Although BCPL produces very efficient and compact code, it is often possible to achieve even more economy by writing some parts of a program, particularly inner loops, in assembler code. This is particularly true if there are features of the hardware that are not envisaged on the BCPL library for that implementation. Because BCPL is designed for segmentation it is quite easy to incorporate segments written in assembler.

The name of the assembler segment is expressed as a global; and space must be reserved for it in the global vector. The assembler must produce an object file with the same format as those produced by the BCPL compiler. This is not difficult, since there will probably be a standard general format for all object files handled by the system. The main special requirement is that global information shall be in the same form as in the BCPL segments. If the assembled code needs to pick up parameters or return a function value it will generally have to refer to the BCPL stack. Typically the stack pointer is held in one of the fast registers. The assembler segment must also take care not to overwrite permanently any registers that the implementation preserves over a routine call (including the BCPL stack pointer).

Confining all code interludes to one or more separate segments involves separate assembler and compiler runs; but some implementations permit the user to introduce a piece of code into the middle of a BCPL block. Typically this is achieved through an additional command CODE that calls the assembler direct. For this to work, the BCPL compiler must incorporate the assembler as part of itself, with a consequent increase in its size.

3.10 FINALLY

BCPL was designed to be a simplification of CPL. The principal simplification was to accept only one data type. Another was to restrict the visible scope of dynamic variables to the "home" block. Since there are no compound data types in BCPL, there are no arrays as such; but the use of the "contents" operator is extended to permit indexed access to a range of memory addresses. The power of BCPL is thus less than that of CPL; but there are compensations. The compiler works fast, and yields fast code; and source programs are clear and concise, with several shorthand features to make them even neater. BCPL also has a small but well defined library of useful functions and routines.

When you are programming in BCPL you should remember that it is a language in which practically anything is legal, if not sensible. This fact arises principally because it is typeless; so you can mix together integers, character codes, vector elements, sections of strings, or pointers to any of these, and the compiler will not say you nay. Some compilers, mainly on larger systems, issue warnings when you do some of the things that might arise from error; but with no data types there is not very much that a compiler can check.

BCPL depends to a greater extent than practically any other language on sound logical thinking by the programmer, and on an understanding of the mechanisms underlying the language. Pointers are a common source of difficulty; so is vector indexing, since you are unlikely to find a check on array bounds. Your best plan is to take the same attitude to your program that you would if you were writing in assembler, treating BCPL merely as a means of writing certain assembly idioms more succinctly.

Chapter 4

Programming Examples in BCPL

The examples that follow are intended to illustrate the techniques discussed in the foregoing three chapters. They have deliberately been kept simple to avoid confusing any issues, and are therefore not offered in any sense as finished pieces of software. Because BCPL is so economical both in compiler needs and in the needs of the object program, it has become particularly popular with users of personal and hobby computers. We have therefore chosen a typical micro system for testing these examples, the Sinclair QL using the Metacomco compiler. Since all versions of BCPL are different, these programs are not portable between systems. But we have tried so far as is practicable to avoid features, which, while they might improve efficiency, are system-specific; and we have tried to write the programs in such a way that they should be relatively easy to modify to the requirements of another system. Certain system-dependent considerations, such as window management, have been left out entirely, even though they would be essential in marketable programs.

4.1 ACKERMANN'S FUNCTION

Ackermann's function is a cliché; but it is useful for several reasons. One is that it makes a good benchmark, another that it illustrates recursion rather well. It is a recursive function that cannot be expressed in a simple *primitive recursive* scheme. Its full definition is:

```
A(0, n) = n + 1
A(m, 0) = A(m−1, 1)
A(m, n) = A(m−1, A(m, n−1))
```

In this example the recursive definition is translated direct into BCPL. Because of multiple recursion the algorithm uses a lot of stack; so a system option should be taken to increase the stack allocation. With the Metacomco compiler this option is offered when the object program is linked to the run-time system.

```
GET "LIBHDR"

LET A(M,N) = M=0 → N+1, N=0 → A(M−1,1), A(M−1, A(M, N−1))
```

51

```
AND START() BE
$(
                LET M, N = 0, 0
                $(
                        WRITES("Type two arguments (zero to exit)*N")
                        M := READN()
                        N := READN()
                        WRITEF(Ackermann(%N, %N) = %N*N", M, N,
                                A(M,N))
                $)REPEATUNTIL M=0
$)
```

4.2   A FASTER ALGORITHM

This second version of Ackermann's function illustrates vectors in
BCPL. It incorporates a speed-up technique in which a two-dimensional
array is used to retain values already computed, so that they can be
retrieved by a simple look-up. Notice that, because of the rule that a
BCPL function has no access to variables declared in outer blocks, the
array must be passed to the Ackermann function as an additional
argument.

```
GET "LIBHDR"

MANIFEST $( maxn = 100 $)

LET A(T,M,N) = VALOF
$(
                LET x = M < 4 & N < maxn → T!(M*maxn + N), 0
                IF x = 0 THEN
                $(
                        TEST M = 0 THEN x := N+1
                        ELSE x := N = 0 → A(T, M−1, 1), A(T, M−1,
                                A(T, M, N−1))
                        IF M<4 & N<maxn THEN T!(M*maxn + N) := x
                $)
                RESULTIS x
$)

AND START() BE
$(
```

```
LET V = VEC 4*maxn
LET M, N = 0, 0
$(
      FOR j = 0 TO 4*maxn DO V!j := 0 //clear array
      WRITES("Type two arguments (zero to exit)*N")
      M := READN()
      N := READN()
      WRITEF("Ackermann(%N,  %N)  =  %N*N", M,  N,
            A(V,M,N)
$) REPEATUNTIL M=0
$)
```

4.3   A SCREEN PAGER

This program displays a selected character file on the screen page by
page. The file name is typed in the normal way and the first page is
displayed. The space bar gets you the next page; the RETURN key
scrolls a single line; the ESCAPE key can be used to exit. readfilename is
implemented as a function for the sake of future development.

```
GET "LIBHDR"

MANIFEST $( nlines = 16 $) // page length

LET oneline(file) BE
$(
            LET c = 0
            SELECTINPUT(file)
            $(
                  c := RDCH()
                  WRCH(c)
                  IF c = '*N' RETURN
                  IF c = ENDSTREAMCH FINISH
            $) REPEAT
$)

AND onepage(file) BE
$(
            FOR count = 1 TO nlines DO oneline(file)
$)
```

```
AND readfilename(n) = VALOF
// reads a name of up to 20 characters into string n
$(
            LET v = VEC 21
            LET j = 1
            $(
                  v!j := RDCH()
                  IF v!j = '*N' BREAK
                  j := j+1
            $) REPEATUNTIL j = 21
            v!0 := j−1
            PACKSTRING(v, n)
            RESULTIS j − 1
$)

AND START() BE
$(
            LET name = VEC 6
            LET file, kbd = 0, 0
            SCREEN(screen.clear) // QL library routine
            kbd := FINDINPUT("con")
            // for QL to get unbuffered input
            WRITES("File name?*N")
            readfilename(name)
            file := FINDINPUT(name)
            onepage(file)
            $(1
                  SELECTINPUT(kbd)
                  SWITCHON RDCH() INTO
                  $(
                        CASE '*N': oneline(file); ENDCASE
                        CASE '*S': onepage(file); ENDCASE
                        CASE 27: FINISH // escape key
            $)1 REPEAT
$)
```

4.4 A SORTING PROGRAM

This is a two-module program that uses modularity to provide a data-independent sorting scheme. The sorting proper is contained in one module, which uses the heapsort algorithm, building a binary tree, inserting items in topological order as they arrive, and printing it out again to give the sorted sequence. This module is data-independent, all manipulation of the data being confined to the other module. Communication between the two is achieved by means of four global routines: initdata, keycomp, getitem and putitem. Any complex set of data items can be used with the same sort module by writing a suitable data module. The data provided for testing is a simple set of random numbers in the range 0 to 511. The example also illustrates how memory blocks are acquired from a free heap, using the function GETVEC. Without this facility, full data independence would have been difficult to achieve.

```
// myhdr: header for heapsort

GET "LIBHDR"

MANIFEST $( nitems = 70 $)

GLOBAL $(
            initdata: 100
            keycomp: 101
            getitem: 102
            putitem: 103
        $)

// This module executes the heapsort algorithm

GET "myhdr"

STATIC $(
            left = 0
            right = 0
        $)

LET insert(k, n) BE
// insert data item k into the tree
// rooted at the position of item n
$(
```

```
                TEST keycomp(k, n) THEN
                        TEST left!n = 0 THEN left!n := k
                        ELSE insert(k, left!n)
                ELSE TEST right!n = 0 THEN right!n := k
                        ELSE insert(k, right!n)
$)


AND puttree(n) BE
// print tree rooted at item n
$(
                IF left!n NE 0 THEN puttree(left!n)
                putitem(n)
                IF right!n NE 0 THEN puttree(right!n)
$)


AND START() BE
$(
                LET L = VEC nitems
                LET R = VEC nitems
                left, right := L, R
                initdata()
                FOR k=0 TO nitems−1 DO
                $(
                        getitem(k)
                        left!k, right!k := 0, 0
                        putitem(k)
                        IF k THEN insert(k, 0)
                $)
                puttree(0)
$)


// This module provides simple test data for heapsort

GET "myhdr"

STATIC $( data = 0 $)

LET initdata() BE data := GETVEC(nitems)

AND keycomp(k, n) = data!k < data!n
```

```
AND getitem(k) BE
$(
            STATIC $( seed = 0 $)
            seed := RANDOM(seed)
            data!k := seed & #777
$)


AND putitem(k) BE
//write ten to a line
$(
            STATIC $( count = 0 $)
            WRITEN(data!k); WRCH('*S')
            count := count+1
            IF count = 10 THEN
                    $( count := 0; NEWLINE() $)
$)
```

4.5 ANOTHER ARRANGEMENT

The previous program made use of a facility for claiming a vector from free memory. Since not all versions of BCPL provide this facility, which in any case the purist might argue is unnecessary, we offer an alternative arrangement that uses the standard function APTOVEC to provide space to hold the data for sorting. The START routine has now to be moved to the data module. What was previously the body of the START routine becomes the routine heapsort. In this arrangement the size of the data set can be varied up to an upper limit

```
// myhdr: header for heapsort

GET "LIBHDR"

MANIFEST $( bigenough = 100 $) //max no of items

GLOBAL $(
            initdata : 100
            keycomp : 101
            getitem : 102
            putitem : 103
            heapsort : 104
        $)
```

```
// This is the heapsort data module

GET "myhdr"

LET keycomp(k, n, V) = (V!k < V!n)

AND getitem(k, V) BE
$(
          STATIC $( seed = 0 $)
          seed := RANDOM(seed)
          V!k := seed & #777
$)

AND putitem(k, V) BE
$(
          STATIC $( count = 0 $)
          WRITEN(V!k); WRCH('*S'); count := count+1
          IF count = 10 THEN $( count := 0; NEWLINE() $)
$)

AND START() BE
$(
          LET nitems = 100
          WRITEF("How many items? (max. %N) *N", bigenough)
          nitems := READN()
          APTOVEC(heapsort, nitems)
$)

// This module executes the heapsort algorithm proper

GET "myhdr"

STATIC $(
          left = 0
          right = 0
       $)

LET insert(k, n, V) BE
// insert data item k into the tree
// rooted at the position of item n
$(
```

```
        TEST keycomp(k, n, V) THEN
            TEST left!n = 0 THEN left!n := k
            ELSE insert(k, left!n, V)
        ELSE TEST right!n = 0 THEN right!n := k
            ELSE insert(k, right!n, V)
$)

AND puttree(n, V) BE
// print tree rooted at item n
$(
        IF left!n NE 0 THEN puttree(left!n, V)
        putitem(n, V)
        IF right!n NE 0 THEN puttree(right!n, V)
$)

AND heapsort(V, n) BE
$(
        LET L = VEC bigenough
        LET R = VEC bigenough
        left, right := L, R
        FOR k=0 TO n−1 DO
        $(
            getitem(k, V)
            left!k, right!k := 0, 0
            putitem(k, V)
            insert(k, 0, V)
        $)
        puttree(0, V)
$)
```

4.6   A SIMPLE TEXT JUSTIFIER

In this example we illustrate how to handle strings in BCPL. The command takes text from a named input file, cuts it into lines of a selectable length (ignoring existing newlines) and delivers it to a select-able output device or file. Optionally the text may be padded out to justify the right margin. A QL quirk is that the keyboard cannot provide an endfile signal when unbuffered. The 255 character is used here to denote the end of keyboard input.

```
    GET "LIBHDR"
```

```
STATIC $(
        k = 0; l = 0 // text pointers
        c = 0 // last character read
        doadjust = 0; end = 0 // flags
        ll = 70 // line length
        invec = 0 // input text
        outvec = 0 // output text
        buffer = 0 // output string
    $)


LET readfilename(s) = VALOF
// read up to 20 characters into string s
$(
        LET v = VEC 21
        AND j = 1
        $(
            v!j := RDCH()
            IF v!j = '*N' BREAK
            j := j + 1
        $) REPEATUNTIL j = 21
        !v := j - 1
        PACKSTRING(v, s)
        RESULTIS j - 1
$)


AND getword() = VALOF
// next word from input stream
// return its length
$(
        LET count = 0
        // ignore leading spaces
        c := RDCH() REPEATWHILE c = ' ' | c = '*N' | c = '*T'
        IF c = ENDSTREAMCH | c = 255 THEN RESULTIS 0
        // 255 is used to end keyboard stream
        $(
            count := count + 1
            invec!count := c
            c := RDCH()
        $) REPEATUNTIL c = '*S' | c = '*N' | c = '*T' |
            c = ENDSTREAMCH | c = 255
        RESULTIS count
$)
```

```
AND copyword(k)
// transfer word of length k from input to output vector
$(
          FOR j = 1 TO k DO outvec!(l + j) := invec!j
          l := l + k + 1
          outvec!l := '*S'
$)


AND adjust(n) BE
// pad output with n extra spaces starting from the right
$(
          !outvec := ll
          WHILE n > 0 DO
              FOR j = ll − n TO 1 BY −1 DO
                  IF outvec!j = '*S' & outvec!(j+1) NE '*S'
                  THEN // move text up
                  $(
                      FOR k = ll TO j+1 BY −1 DO
                          outvec!k := outvec!(k−1)
                      n := n − 1
                      IF n < 1 RETURN
                  $)
$)


AND START() BE
$(
          LET V = VEC 30
          AND W = VEC 100
          AND S = VEC 25
          AND name = VEC 5
          AND source = FINDINPUT("con")
          // default for QL buffered input
          AND destin = SYSOUT // default output
          invec, outvec, buffer := V, W, S
          SCREEN(screen.clear) // QL routine
          WRITES("Input file?*N")
          IF readfilename(name) > 0 THEN
              source := FINDINPUT(name)
          WRITES("Output file?*N")
          IF readfilename(name) > 0 THEN
              destin := FINDOUTPUT(name)
```

```
WRITES("Adjust Y/N   ")
c := RDCH()
IF c = 'y' | c = 'Y' THEN doadjust := 1
RDCH() // ignore newline after Y/N
WRITES("Line length? (max 100)   ")
IF RDCH() NE '*N' THEN // default if newline
$(
      UNRDCH()
      ll := READN()
$)
`SELECTINPUT(source)
SELECTOUTPUT(destin)
// end of preamble
      $(
            k := getword
            IF c = ENDSTREAMCH | c = 255 THEN end := 1
            TEST k <= ll - l THEN copyword(k)
            ELSE // line full, write it
            $(
                  outvec!0 := l - 1
                  IF doadjust THEN adjust(ll-l+1)
                  PACKSTRING(outvec, buffer)
                  WRITES(buffer)
                  NEWLINE()
                  l := 0
                  copyword(k)
            $)
      $) REPEATUNTIL end
      // write remaining text if any
      IF l THEN
      $(
            outvec!0 := l - 1
            PACKSTRING(outvec, buffer)
            WRITES(buffer)
            NEWLINE()
      $)
$)
$)
```

Chapter 5

A Brief Look at B

B, like BCPL, is a typeless (or if you prefer it a single-type) language, all manipulations being on an implementation-dependent "word" that may represent an integer, a logical quantity, a bit string, a short sequence of characters, or an address. As in BCPL the only compound object permitted is a one-dimensional vector of words. B does however incorporate floating point, which is implemented in an untyped manner by providing a set of distinct operators that perform specialised operations on what are in effect short word vectors. Apart from its typeless character however, and the implications that follow from that, B has more in common with C than with BCPL. The conventions of its syntax are similar to those of C, even extending to the use of identical symbols for identical purposes; and its run-time library foreshadows many of the features of the C library.

In common with the other languages described here, B is designed for separate compilation. It achieves this aim not with the aid of a global vector like BCPL, but in the conventional way by linking like C. A program in B consists of a set of *modules*. A B module is not, as might be thought, an individual file but a distinct object presented to the compiler. Thus several modules may reside upon a single file. Modules are of three types:

> manifest constants,
> external variables,
> function definitions.

Files may also contain compiler directives. These are lines starting with #; and are used in the main for annotating any object cards produced by the program. File inclusion is normally part of the operating system.

5.1 CONSTANTS

Constants can be numeric quantities, characters, or strings. Integer quantities are normally interpreted as decimal; though a constant starting with zero is taken to be octal. Any of the usual representations may be used to define floating-point constants, the presence of a point ensuring that a number is interpreted in this form.

Character constants are written between single quotes. Since the only data type in B is the word, a character constant may include several individual characters up to the length of a word. Where the constant contains fewer characters than would fit into a full word, they are right-adjusted and left-padded with zeros. The ASCII code is presumed; but the interpretation of characters in a shorter "BCD" form can be forced by prefacing the constant with a $. This feature will normally appear only on machines with 6-bit character form.

Strings are written between double quotes. Characters are packed, typically four to a word, and the string is terminated, as in C, by a null character. There is no length count as there is in BCPL, so the length of a string is not limited by the language. Non-print codes, and characters used for special purposes, are escaped with an asterisk. Thus *n is a newline, *0 a null, and ** the code for an asterisk. The same escape character is used in making up characters, such as braces, which do not feature on all keyboards. For instance *(is a legitimate alternative to {.

A *manifest* constant is essentially a simple macro definition of the form

    name=text

The compiler (or its preprocessor) then replaces every subsequent occurrence of that name by the associated text, which may be a simple constant or a string or indeed any piece of program text. Names defined earlier can appear in the text of subsequent manifest constants to a system-defined depth. The facility is thus rather like the #define facility in C, but without parameterisation.

5.2   EXTERNAL DEFINITIONS

All names declared, and optionally initialised, outside a function body are treated as external. There are no static quantities in B, except of course for labels. The declaration

    count {25}

allocates one word, initialises it to the value between the braces, and adds the name "count" to the external symbol table.

The declaration

    table[25]

using square brackets, creates a vector. B, like BCPL, creates vectors one cell longer than the number given as the dimension. Thus the vector referred to here as "table" is of length 26, and is indexed from 0 to 25. It is uninitialised, except that table[0] is set to zero.

An initialised vector can be created like a scalar, thus

months {31, 28, 31, 30, 31, 30, 31, 31, 30, 31, 30, 31}

Strings too are vectors, and are similarly declared: for instance

message { "ring me tomorrow" }

As a result of these two declarations the names months and message would be associated with pointers that designate the locations of the first word of each of the two vectors.

An alternative way to declare an initialised vector is

months[] {31, 28, 31, 30, 31, 30, 31, 31, 30, 31, 30, 31}

In this declaration months is not a pointer but names directly the first cell. If no dimension is given, the compiler allocates enough space to accommodate all the initialisers. If a dimension is specified that is longer than the number of initialisers, then only the lower-indexed cells are initialised. If the dimension is insufficient, then it is ignored.`

Arrays of strings can be created similarly.

rhyme[] { "mary", "mary", "quite", "contrary", −1 }

sets up an array of pointers, the first four designating strings, the last taking the value −1. It is normal practice in B to use −1 to terminate string arrays in this way. The individual strings are as usual null-terminated.

Multidimensional arrays can be declared as vectors of vectors, and are accessed in the form a[i][j]. They can be initialised if necessary row-by-row, using nested pairs of braces. This is all in a style later to be adopted in C.

5.3   FUNCTIONS

As in C, there is no distinction in B between declaring routines that return a value and declaring ones that do not. A return statement with a predicate, embedded in the function body, operates like RESULTIS in BCPL by causing the value of that predicate to be returned. If the return is unpredicated, or if a return occurs simply because control has come to the end of the function body, then the returned value is undefined and should be ignored. All function names are treated as external.

The general form of a function declaration is

name(argument list) statement

The argument list may be empty; but brackets are still required. Arguments are passed by value; though by passing a pointer you can achieve the equivalent of a call by reference. This is the normal means whereby a function can be induced to accept an array or a string or another function as an "argument". In B as in BCPL a function call can specify fewer arguments than are to be found in the function definition. The parameter-passing mechanism is similar to the initialisation of a vector, so cells on the stack are initialised in sequence from the first, the function text supplying default values if necessary. A library function nargs() can be used to compute the actual number of arguments supplied.

External names are made accessible within a function body by redeclaring them in the form

extrn namelist

Apart from externals and formal arguments, the only other names accessible inside a function body are labels and automatic variables. A label is a name followed by a colon. It precedes either a statement or another label. Its value is the location of the start of the code representing the labelled statement. A label is thus the only static object in B.

Automatic (or local) variables are declared in the form

auto list

The list can contain either simple names or names followed by a constant in square brackets. A simple name causes a single word to be allocated on the stack. If the name is followed by a bracketed constant, then two more cells are allocated than the value of the constant, providing space for a vector of length one more than the constant, and a pointer to its first element. The result is similar to that of the VEC operator in BCPL.

One function must be named main. It is this function to which control is passed initially by the run-time system. Two arguments may be passed to main These are argc and argv. argv is a vector of pointers to strings; and argc gives its dimension, as if it had been declared (illegally, since argc is not a constant) as argv[argc]. The strings pointed to by argv are derived from the command line that calls the executable program, the command itself (normally the program name) being argv[0].

5.4 EXPRESSIONS

B provided all the operators later adopted for C, with the exception of the comma operator. They can be found tabulated in order of binding power in chapter 7 In contrast to the convention in BCPL, assignment in B, and subsequently in C, is not a type of statement but an operator. There are a number of assignment operators, giving a variety of "two-address" operations, both arithmetic and logical, a typical one being

    x += y

which assigns the sum of x and y to y. There is also an incrementation operator ++ and a decrementation operator −−, both of which imply assignment. Incrementation and decrementation can be made to operate either before or after a variable has been used in a larger expression.

   In common with the other languages considered here, B explicitly recognises the distinction between the right value and the left value associated with a variable name. Which of these two is taken in a particular situation depends on the context. The addressing operator & forces the use of the left value in a situation where a right value would normally be taken. For instance

    x = &y

assigns the *address* of y to x. The contents operator ∗ does the converse. Thus

    ∗x = y

takes the contents of x as the address of a cell to which the right value of y is to be copied.

5.5 FLOATING POINT

Certain arithmetic and relational operators can be prefaced with a "hash" sign, which makes them applicable to floating-point variables. There is no floating incrementation or decrementation; and only simple assignment can be used with floating-point operands. Nor may integers and floating-point quantities be mixed in expressions in the ordinary way. However, the unary operator # returns the floating-point equivalent of an integer operand; and the unary operator ## returns the integer equivalent of a floating-point operand. The precision of floating point is defined by the implementation.

5.6 STATEMENTS

In B, as in C, the semicolon is used as a statement terminator, not a separator. A semicolon alone makes a null statement; and any expression can be made into a statement by writing a semicolon after it, the expression's value then being discarded. A sequence of statements enclosed in braces constitutes a compound statement, which is syntactically equivalent to a single statement. Syntactically too declarations using extern and auto are treated as statements, and may appear anywhere in a block.

Simple transfer of control is achieved with return, break, next or goto. return has already been discussed. break takes control from inside a loop or switch to the statement following. next is equivalent to BCPL LOOP and C continue. It forces an immediate attempt to reiterate. goto in B, as in C, can take only a label, not, as in BCPL, a general left-value expression.

The conditional statement takes the same form as in C, viz.

> if (expression) statement

or   if (expression) statement else statement

The controlled statements may of course be conditional themselves; in which case the rule is that else associates with its *nearest* precedent if. The expression will normally make use of relational and Boolean operators; but B treats any nonzero value as "true" and zero as "false"; so the expression may be a simple variable, or a purely arithmetic expression.

There are four forms of iterative statement in B; and these correspond exactly with what was later provided in C. They are

> repeat statement

which requires a break or return for escape,

> while (expression) statement

and   do statement while (expression)

the last providing at least one execution of the controlled statement.

Though not strictly necessary, The iterative structure

> for (exp1; exp2; exp3) statement

is made available principally for constructing a conventional counting loop. "exp1" is executed before entry to thr loop, "exp3" is executed repeatedly at the end of each cycle; and iteration continues so long as "exp2" returns nonzero.

Finally B has a switch statement whose general form has been carried through into C. There are however one minor and one major difference between the B and C syntax. The minor difference is that multiple labels in B must be separated by double colons. The major difference is that a case constant in B may be preceded by a relational operator, as for instance

    case >= midvalue: . . . .

It is not clear why this most useful facility was not made available in C.

5.7 THE B LIBRARY

The library provided with B foreshadows the more extensive library of C. It offers a compromise between the BCPL idea of switching a "current" input and output channel and the C idea of designating one input and one output channel as "standard", and allowing several other channels to be accessible simultaneously. In B the current channels are opened initially to default devices by the system; but on most implementations they may be redirected during execution.

B, like both BCPL and C, operates on data streams for both input and output. Like C it provides alternative input and output functions to handle the standard channels and the rest. The functions getchar and getc return the next single character respectively from the standard input and from an arbitrary input channel supplied as an argument. Functions putchar and putc perform similar operations in the opposite sense. There is also a function ungetc, as in C and some versions of BCPL, which puts a character back into the last position read. It is worth noting by the way that, when B was first developed, standard input was likely to have been a punched-card reader and standard output a line printer.

Because B allows a variable number of arguments to be passed to a function, there is strictly no necessity to have separate functions to operate on the default and other channels. Indeed the other transput functions do not. In the function

    getstring(channel, string, maxl)

only the second argument is mandatory. The default channel is standard input. Taking the option to specify a maximum length, maxl, for the string can prevent a crash if the string exceeds the space allotted for it. Input by getstring terminates at the next newline, which is not stored. An alternative function getline is provided in case it is wished to store the newline. Both these functions store a terminating null. There is also a function reread that sets the buffer pointer back to the beginning of the current line.

There is a function putstring for outputting text. The whole string is output (except for the terminating null), whether or not it contains newlines. getnum and putnum are provided for the conversion and transput of numeric quantities; but there is also a general formatted output function printf that works like printf in C and WRITEF in BCPL. Some implementations also provide a formatted input function.

Channels other than the default standard ones are created by the function

    open(filename, mode)

This returns an integer that is used to "name" the channel in future references to it. The filename is a system-dependent string; and "mode", also a string, determines whether the channel is to be read or written, and whether it is sequential or random. Random files can also be opened in read-write mode, and sequential files in append mode.

For random input there is a function

    read(channel, buffer, sector, nwds)

The buffer here is defined by a pointer. "sector" indicates where on the device reading should start; and "nwds" specifies the number of words to transfer. There is also a random write function with similar arguments. These return the number of words transferred; but in cases of error they return a (negative) error code.

5.8   STRING HANDLING

A few functions are provided to perform special operations on word sequences containing packed character codes. The arguments to them should be pointers. nullstring tests whether its argument points to a null string; length returns the length of a string; and equal compares two strings for equality, though it may not indicate which is lexicographically greater.

    concat(dest, s1, s2 ....)

catenates a set of strings, placing the result in "dest", which may be the same as "s1". There is also a function getarg that was originally designed for separating string arguments. This can be used to move strings from place to place. When using getarg and concat it is the reponsibility of the programmer to ensure that string destinations do not overflow.

There are functions in B like the BCPL getbyte and putbyte for selecting, or changing, an individual character in a string if its index is known. However there is another method of processing strings that is usually faster. B permits strings to be opened for reading, writing, or appending just like sequential files; this allows them to be processed character by character using putc and getc, or in larger pieces with putstring and getstring.

5.9   MEMORY ALLOCATION

B is implemented in such a way that it is able to obtain extra memory during execution. This may come as the result of an operating system call; or it may come from a reserve held by the B run-time controller. A program gets more memory by using the function getvec, the argument of which is the number of words requested. getvec returns a pointer to the new memory area, which is normally then assigned to an external variable. When the space is no longer required it should be released by the call

    rlsevec(ptr, n)

which releases n words starting at the contents of "ptr". It is the programmer's responsibility to remember and quote the size of each block released. The B system does not keep a record of block sizes as does C.

Chapter 6

C Declarations and Structure

Variables, functions, and named constants in C are referred to by *identifiers*, which start with a letter and may include letters, numerals and the underscore character. In some implementations the full stop and dollar sign too may be used. Letters in identifiers are case-sensitive, i.e. dog and Dog are different identifiers. Only the first eight characters of an identifier are significant in most implementations.

In contrast to BCPL and B, C is a *typed* language. The basic type specifiers are char, int, float, and double. Integers may be further characterised as short, long or unsigned. The facility for specifying unsigned integers is mainly of importance when operands are multiplied or divided; though, on machines that do not use twos-complement representation, even addition and subtraction may give different results on signed and unsigned operands.

The number of bits assigned to each of these types is machine-dependent, which means that C programs may not be portable between machines unless certain precautions have been taken. However, forward portability should be guaranteed between different implementations of UNIX, and even between implementations of UNIX and XENIX. Typically short and long are represented by 16 and 32 bits respectively, while float and double are represented respectively by 32 and 64 bits. The length assigned to int and unsigned is that of the system "word", i.e. the data item that is most efficiently handled by the hardware. The type specifiers long int, short int and unsigned int are permissible alternatives, while long float is taken as an equivalent of double. unsigned short and unsigned long also are usually available. long, int, short and also char (see below) are designated *integer types*, and may be mixed in expressions.

6.1 CHARACTERS AND STRINGS

Type char is usually, but not always, represented by an 8-bit byte. Some implementations treat characters as signed quantities (typically in the range -128 to 127). In such cases unsigned char is available as an alternative type.

A character constant is written between single quotes, as 'a'. Its numeric value depends on the character code being used, which is normally ASCII. A *string* constant is a sequence of zero or more characters enclosed between *double* quotes, as for instance

   "this is a string"

Physically a string is represented as an array of type char. Its first byte contains the code for the first character not, as in BCPL, the string's length. This is determined by the position of a terminating null (zero) byte; so there is no limit in the language (in contrast to a particular implementation) to the length of a string.

   You can use non-printable codes in strings, or individually as characters, by escaping with a backslash. Thus /n represents a newline, /t a tab, /b a backspace, /r a carriage return, and /f a form-feed (page throw). An arbitrary bit pattern can be represented as a backslash followed by up to three octal digits, or in most implementations by /x or /X and up to two hexadecimal digits. As a special case of this, the terminating null character can be represented as /0, though naturally it cannot appear in the body of a string. Some implementations allow /e for the escape code (decimal 27 in ASCII). The metacharacters used in string and character representaion can be represented as themselves by escaping with a backslash. Thus you can use /', /", and // to represent respectively single and double quotes and a backslash in character constants and strings.

6.2 NUMBERS

Numeric constants are written according to the normal conventions. If a point is included, then a constant is taken to be in floating point, and is stored in *double* precision. The "E" or "e" notation for floating point is also permissible, e.g. 98.765E43. Integer constants that are small enough are stored as type int, whether this be equivalent to long or short. Where int is not equivalent to long, a constant can be forced to be stored as long by writing L immediately after it. Constants are normally taken to be decimal. A leading zero indicates an octal constant; and a leading 0X or 0x indicates hexadecimal. a to f can be used as alternatives to A to F in hexadecimal numbers. A trailing L can also be used to indicate long octal or hexadecimal constants. Hexadecimal and octal constants are stored as *unsigned*.

6.3 DECLARATIONS

Every data item in C must be *declared* before it can be referred to in an expression. A declaration consists of four parts:

storage class,
type specifier,
declarator,
initialiser,

and must be terminated by a semicolon. The semicolon is always a *terminator* in C, not a separator as it is in certain other languages. The storage class, the type specifier, and the initialiser may be omitted. When the type specification is omitted, the type is presumed to be int.

For the present we shall confine our remarks to declarations that involve simple scalar variables. The initialiser for a scalar can be any sort of expression, provided that the identifiers used in it are all *visible* at the point of declaration, and provided that type conflict does not arise. We define the term *visibility* in the next paragraph. You can put several declarators of the same type in a single declaration; and any or all may be initialised. Thus any of the following could be legal declarations:

```
float x, y, z=3.45 ;
count = 0, max = A + ext, min = A - ext ;
tom ;
char C = '/0';
```

In the first example, x and y are uninitialised. In the second tom is taken to be type int; though some compilers will insist on the word int appearing explicitly in certain contexts.

6.4 STORAGE CLASS

When a data item is declared, it acquires a characteristic known as its *visibility*, which is the part of the program over which it may legitimately be referred to. The term *scope* is used by some authorities; though this term is ambiguous, since it is sometimes used to denote the part of the program over which storage for a variable remains in existence. This last we refer to as the variable's *lifespan*. Lifespan and visibility are determined by the *storage class* of an item.

As in all block-structured languages, data declared inside a C block has no existence outside, and ceases to exist when control leaves the block. Its *lifespan* is therefore that of the block, and its visibility is the remainder of the block between its declaration and the end. Such data is said to be *automatic*. The specifier auto may be used to preface the declaration; but if the specifier is omitted the variable is automatically taken to be automatic, and space is not allocated for it until the block is entered.

Variables may also be declared at the top level, i.e. outside any function declaration. Such variables are either *static* or *external*. C was designed for separate compilation; that is to say a C program can be written, compiled, stored and tested as a set of separate modules that will eventually be linked together for execution. The difference between static and external variables is that the former are visible only from the point of declaration up to the end of the module, while external variables can be made visible in other modules. The lifespan of both is the duration of the program.

Static and external variables thus provide for communication between program blocks in the same or different modules. They may be initialised in the original declaration. If they are not, then C initialises them to zero. This is in contrast to automatic variables, which may get any arbitrary value if they are not initialised. An item declared at the top level and not specifically declared to be static is treated as external.

External items are not automatically visible in other modules. They must be made so by means of a *reference*, which must appear in every module where the variable is to be made visible. Typical external references are

```
extern no_of_users, runtime, is_running ;
extern double maxerror ;
```

Most compilers require extern to be omitted in the original declaration, and used only in references. It is common practice to keep all the references for a whole program, together with other common material, in a header file. This can then be included at the start of the text of every module in the program.

Variables declared within blocks can also have the static or external storage class, for instance

```
static char ch ;
static float range ;
```

One reason for declaring static variables within blocks is to ensure that certain values are retained between one activation of the block and the next.

If a name is visible over only part of a program, we can use it to identify a different object in a different context. This practice is called *overloading*. A name may be overloaded if it is used in different visible regions; but there are other kinds of overloading too, which we shall discuss when we come to them.

6.5 OTHER STORAGE CLASSES

It is possible to achieve appreciable improvements in the speed of object code if certain critical items such as stack pointers are held in the machine's fast registers. C therefore provides the storage class register. A variable declared to be in this class will be treated in all other respects as an automatic item, except that it will be held in one of the machine's fast registers (*provided that* one is available) and not, as is usual with automatic items, on the working stack. The rules for using the register specifier are system dependent. For instance registers in some machines are too short to accommodate longer types, though many modern microprocessors allow registers to hold any length of word from 8 to 64 bits.

Some implementors treat formal arguments in function definitions as a separate storage class formal. However, in general formal items are treated in the same way as automatic items, except that they are not initialised until the function is called.

The keyword typedef counts syntactically as a storage class; but it does not allocate storage. Instead it associates a name with a particular storage type. It can be used to assist portability when equivalent types have different representations on different systems; for instance

```
typedef unsigned char byte
```

establishes a type byte, which is equivalent to unsigned char. typedef can also be used to establish a shorthand form for complex declarations, and thus improve readability. We shall have more to say about defining new types when we come to deal with pointers and structures. An instance appears among the programming examples in chapter 10.

6.6 RIGHT VALUES AND LEFT VALUES

In a simple assignment such as

```
x = y
```

the names x and y are treated differently. While y on the right of the assignment is evaluated to give the *content* of the memory cell associated with it, x on the left is evaluated to yield the address of the cell itself. The assignment is achieved by placing a copy of the value associated with y in the x location. We therefore refer to names as having both a *right value* and a *left value*.

There is in C an operator that enables a variable on the right-hand side of an assignment to be evaluated to its left value. This uses the ampersand symbol & . The assignment

    x = &z

would put not the right value of z but its *address* into the location associated with x. The resulting situation might be represented diagrammatically as

x is then said to contain a *pointer* to z. & is known as the *address operator*. It can be applied legitimately only to something that is able to yield a left value. For instance, it would be nonsensical to write &(x + y), where x and y are numeric types, or &25. It is also illegal to apply & to a register variable.

By symmetry, C also provides a right-value operator. This is ∗ . The assignment

    w = ∗x

would assign to w the same value as would the assignment

    w = z

assuming that x had been defined as above. ∗ is known as the *contents* or *indirection* operator; and its use before a pointer variable is called *dereferencing*. Because it is the inverse of the address operator, writing ∗&x is equivalent to writing simply x. & and ∗ are both unary (monadic) operators; we shall see later that both & and ∗ are used as dyadic operators as well, but with different meanings.

The declaration

    int ∗p ;

creates a new object of integer type; but it applies the name p not to the object itself but to a pointer to it. It is then possible to make assignments to the object, working through p, thus

    ∗p = 1234 ; or ∗p = q ;

where q in this case should be int or a type that can be coerced to int. The type of p is "pointer to int".

The above assignments place the number 1234 or the right value of q in the cell pointed to by p, i.e. in the cell *p. After the assignment we might show the situation diagrammatically thus:

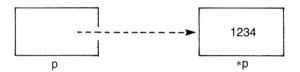

Notice that this situation is very different from that produced by the assignment

   p = 1234 ;

which would treat p itself as int and replace its previous contents by 1234, thus.

```
┌─────────────┐
│             │
│   1234      │
│             │
└─────────────┘
      p
```

Because p exists apart from the integer cell it points to, it can be used as a general-purpose pointer by assigning to it in turn the *addresses* of different objects of type int.

   p = &m ; .... p = &n ;

To assign to it the address of any other type of object must be adjudged an error, though some compilers will allow you to do this; and it is possible to get certain (generally non-portable) effects in this way.

You can of course assign one pointer to another, just as you can assign data objects.

   q = p

given that p and q are both pointers, causes q to point to the object already pointed to by p, thus

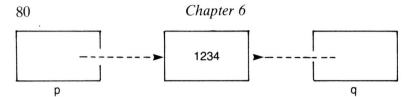

This is quite different from assigning the *contents* of q to that of p, i.e.

> *q = *p

which leads to

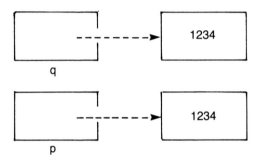

A test for equality between p and q would yield "true" in the first case, "false" in the second; while the same test between *p and *q would yield "true" in both cases.

The indirection operator, * can be applied to any expression that evaluates to a pointer. What this means is that the expression must be either a simple pointer or a pointer increased or decreased by an integer. Thus

> *(p + 4) = z ;

is a legal assignment in C. The expression (p + 4) is evaluated to yield a pointer to the fourth item after that pointed to by p. The value of the expression thus depends on what type (and hence length) of object p points to. We shall see the importance of this later when we deal with arrays.

6.7 ARRAYS

You can declare an array of any C type by placing the dimension in square brackets after the declarator, thus

> float ordinate[25] ;

This creates an array of 25 objects (not 26 as in BCPL) of type float. The dimension can be an expression, provided that it is a *constant* expression; i.e. the value of any symbol used in it must be known at compile time so that space can be allocated statically for the array. It is important to appreciate, though, that ordinate does not name the block of data but a pointer to it. While the data itself is static, the pointer, associated with the identifier ordinate, has a storage class, and hence visibility, depending on the circumstances of the declaration.

It is possible to have an array of arrays, in other words, a two-dimensional array

    static int matrix[12][10];

which may be thought of as having 12 rows and 10 columns according to the normal convention. In other words, matrix is a static pointer to an array of 12 objects, each of which itself is an array of 10 integers. The number of dimensions can be extended up to a system-defined limit; but notice that a separate pair of square brackets is required in most implementations of C for each dimension.

Arrays in C are indexed *from zero*; and an individual array element is selected by writing its index (or indices) in square brackets, e.g.

    ordinate[17]   or   matrix[i][j]

Following normal practice in programming languages, subscript expressions may appear on the left-hand side of assignments, as for instance

    a[i][j] = b[i][k] * c[k][j]

In common with most other languages, C does not allow arrays to be handled *in toto*. This arises from the fact that the array name does not designate the complete array but a pointer to the array's first element. Thus, if a has been declared to be an array, then by definition *a is equivalent to a[0]. It follows that an (entire) array cannot have a left value, though any individual element can.

By extending the definition just given, the expression a[b], where b is of an integer type, becomes a pointer to element b of the array, which is the normal significance of a subscripted expression in other languages. In C the expression *(a + b) is defined to have precisely the same significance. This is a rather special expression, since on the face of it it involves a type conflict, the addition of a pointer and an integer. To make the expression point to element b of the array, it has to be evaluated by first multiplying b by the size of an element of a before performing the addition. The + in this expression is therefore non-commutative.

Since a subscripted expression has the significance of a pointer, the reverse must apply; so any expression with a left value can be subscripted in C. Thus if we declare

```
double *p ;
```

then we may legitimately write p[3]. The effect is to generate a pointer to the third double-sized cell following that pointed to by p, and to take either that pointer or the content of the cell, depending upon the context in which the expression appears.

In C we have a choice of techniques for processing arrays. If we want to visit array elements in sequence, then we can do it either by incrementing an array index, the usual convention in high-level languages, or, as in assembler, by incrementing the array name itself. The latter is usually faster. In this connection we should note that multidimensional arrays in C are stored *by row*. This means that elements stored adjacently usually differ only in their last index except at the end of a row. If an array has been declared as A[m][n], then element A[i][n−1] is followed in storage by element A[i+1][0].

We can define arrays of pointers, and pointers to arrays. The declaration

```
int *rblock[10] ;
```

defines rblock to be an array of pointers to ten objects of type int. In contrast, the declaration

```
int (*iblock)[10] ;
```

declares iblock to be a single pointer to an array of ten integers. In this last case, the first element may be designated as either *iblock[0] or as **iblock. Because the term "array" itself signifies a pointer, we need *double* dereferencing to gain access to the array elements themselves. We shall have occasion to refer to these and similar declarations again in the next chapter when we discuss the binding power (precedence) of operators.

Arrays in C are initialised to zero by default when they are declared. Static or external arrays can be initialised to other values by using a sequence of constant expressions enclosed between braces, thus

```
table[4] = {0, 1, 2, 3} ;
```

Multidimensional arrays should strictly be initialised with the initialisers for the separate rows in braces.

```
matrix[2][3] =
{
{1, 2, 3}
{4, 5, 6}
} ;
```

However, if all the initialisers are present, most compilers will allow you to omit the inner braces. If some initialisers are missing, those given will be assigned by varying the last index most rapidly, resetting an index to zero and incrementing its left-hand neighbour when either the former reaches the limit or a right brace appears.

6.8 STRINGS

A string in C is an array of char. Variable strings can therefore be declared e.g. as

```
char keybuf[128] ;
```

and individual characters can be selected by subscripting. All that we have just been saying about arrays applies equally to strings; in particular, a string name can be treated as a pointer to the first character.

```
char *in = keybuf ;
```

would initialise in to point to the start of the string keybuf, as alternatively would

```
char *in = &keybuf[0] ;
```

String variables can be initialised with string constants. It is not necessary to specify the length when declaring an initialised string, since the compiler can deduce this from the value of the initialiser, thus

```
char message[] = "press return key" ;
```

but you can still do so if you want to create a string variable longer than its initial value, as

```
char buffer[100] = " ";
```

6.9 STRUCTURES

While arrays are the only compound or *aggregate* data type in BCPL and B, C provides structures as well. A structure, like an array, is decomposable into more elementary components. However, it differs from an array in being inhomogeneous. Its components are not all of the same type. In C the components of a structure are referred to as its *members* (the term *field* is used in a different sense in C). Each member of a structure carries an identifier, which is used to gain access to it. Thus we might declare a simple structure as follows:

```
struct card {
        char suit ;
        int faceval ;
        } ;
```

It is important to understand that we are not declaring here an individual data object, as we have been doing in most of the declarations considered up to now, but a template for a new composite data type, which in this case we have associated with the tag card. Having defined the template, we can go on to declare individual objects of the type. We can do this in either of two ways. The simplest is to use the tag as an abbreviation for the full template, thus

```
struct card topofpack ;
struct card tartstealer = {'H', 11} ;
struct card hand[13] ;
struct card *play ;
```

Notice that the specifier struct has to appear in each declaration as well as the tag. The second example shows how structured types are initialised, by putting the initialisers in the appropriate order in braces. The third example shows that you can have arrays of structures; the fourth that you can have pointers to stuctures just as you can to any other type of object. You cannot however have functions that return structures; though there is nothing to prevent a function from returning a *pointer* to a structure.

The other way to declare instances of a structure is to write their names straight after the specification and before the closing semicolon, thus

```
struct card
        {
        char suit ;
        int faceval ;
        }
topofpack, *play, hand[13] ;
```

The declared instances can be initialised in this form of declaration as well. Moreover, if these happen to be the *only* instances of this particular structure, and the template does not have to be used again, there is no need for the tag (in this case card). The type is then said to be *anonymous*.

A structure can be self-referential, i.e. it can be referred to within its own definition. This is essential if, as is commonly the case, structures are to be linked together through the medium of pointers. Consider for example the declaration

```
struct person
        {
        char name[20] ;
        int age ;
        struct person *sibling ;
        struct person *family ;
        }

   ;
```

Here we have a structure that can be connected to other similar structures through two pointers sibling and family. As before, we can declare and initialise instances of the structure:

```
struct person first = {"Adam", 130, NULL, &Cain } ;
```

Notice the use here of the value NULL, which is used to denote that the "sibling" pointer in this case has nothing to point to. NULL is strictly the *only* value that can be common to pointers without regard to the types they point to.

It is possible to initialise arrays of structures by extending the braces to include the initial values for each instance in turn. Consider the following problem. Although all printers use the same standard codes for the letters and numbers and most of the other symbols, there are a few symbols whose codes differ from printer to printer. It would be useful to gather the exceptions in a table so that a print routine could change codes when necessary. The following declaration might therefore be useful:

```
struct
    {
    char internal ;
    int external ;
    } printtab[10] = {
        '`', 0X23,
        '%', 0X3E,
        '{', 0X7B,
        '}', 0X7D }
  ;
```

This declares printtab to be an array of instances of an anonymous structure type, and initialises the first four lines of it. In some implementations you have to put the individual initialisation lines in braces if not all are initialised.

We need to be able to refer to individual members of a structure. This we do by using the dot operator, e.g. after the declaration

```
struct card
    {
    char suit ;
    int faceval ;
    } topofpack, *play, hand[13] ;
```

we may write

```
topofpack.suit      or      topofpack.faceval
```

Member names are used only in the context of one structure type. Because of this most compilers allow them to be overloaded. Thus suit could be used elsewhere in the same program as the name of a scalar variable, or even as another type. Not only this, but it could be used without ambiguity to name a member of another structure type, wardrobe say.

Where we have arrays of structures, we want to be able to refer to the components of individual array elements, for instance we might want to add another line to the structure printtab defined above by writing

```
printtab[4].internal = '`'
printtab[4].external = 6
```

Where we have structure members that are themselves arrays, we want to be able to index them. For example, after the declaration

```
struct order
        {
        char name[15] ;
        char address[40] ;
        int item_no[20] ;
        float item_cost[20] ;
        } next_order ;
```

we might wish to refer to

next_order.item_cost[j]

C provides a further selector operator for structures, −>. This is used instead of the dot operator when we have, as we often do, a pointer to a structure rather than the structure itself. Thus, if play is a pointer to an object of type card, then we can write for instance

play−>suit

This is in fact just another way of writing *play.suit; but it might be judged a little easier to comprehend. The operator −> is very useful for moving down chains of pointers. Thus

Adam.family−>age

should yield the age of Cain, while

Adam.family−>sibling−>name

should yield "Abel".

The members of a structure in C need not be complete computer words, or even bytes. Sometimes it is convenient to pack several small integers, or even one-bit flags, into a single word. Such part words are known as *fields*. In most languages, part-word fields are handled explicitly by using a sequence of mask and shift operators; but C goes further than this, and permits fields to be declared individually as structure members. They can then be handled with the dot and −> operators in the same way as standard-length members.

Fields are typed as unsigned. A colon after a member name in a structure declaration indicates a field. It is followed by the field length in bits. Here is an example

```
struct colour_byte {
        unsigned paper_colour: 3 ;
        unsigned ink_colour: 3 ;
        unsigned is_stippled: 1 ;
        } ;
```

giving the possibility of up to 8 colours. A field length of zero causes the next field to be aligned to the next word boundary. A missing field name causes the specified number of bits to be inserted as a filler.

6.10 UNIONS

Occasionally it is necessary for different types of object to be stored at different times under the same name. For instance, one might have a quantity defining some characteristic of peripheral devices. For simple devices a single integer might suffice to define this characteristic, while for others several integers could be necessary. This problem can be solved by making the quantity in question the union of an integer and a pointer to a subsidiary array of integers.

A union may be thought of as a structure whose members are superimposed instead of being placed end-to-end, and whose length is therefore that of the longest member. Because of its similarity to a structure, a union is specified in exactly the same way, except of course that the word union is used in place of struct. For instance, the union just described might be

```
union {
        int arg ;
        int pargs[4] ;
        } printer_a, tape_a ;
```

Like a structure a union may be given a tag to be used in later references. Unions cannot be initialised; but values can be assigned to them in the same way as to members of structures by using the dot or -> operator. The type of each initialiser has to be explicit in every assignment:

```
printer_a.arg = 128 ;
tape_a.pargs[3] = 1024 ;
```

6.11 ENUMERATIONS

Following the lead of Pascal, a few implementations of C allow the use of enumerations. Thus, instead of defining the suit of a card as a charac-ter, we might define a new type suit as follows

```
enum suit {club, diamond, heart, spade}
```

We can then use the tags club, diamond, etc. as values of type suit just as we use 'C', 'D' etc. as values of type char. Since suit is now a type, we should have to rewrite the delaration of card, which might become

```
struct card
    {
    suit s ;
    int faceval ;
    } *play, hand[13] ;
```

We could then use the values of type suit in expressions, for instance

```
*play->s = heart ;
hand[j].s = spade ;
```

Enumeration values are essentially of type int. This particular enum declaration is really a way of associating 0 with club, 1 with diamond and so on; so you might just as well have written

```
*play->s = 2 ;
hand[j].s = 3 ;
```

if you could remember that heart is 2 and spade 3, and were not concerned about readability. Sequential values from 0 upward are assigned by default. The C implementations that include enumerations often go even further than Pascal by allowing you to define your own enumeration values if you wish. For instance you might define a type

```
enum nonprint = {esc=27, bs=8, lf=10, cr=13, sp=32} ;
```

Of course, as we shall see, you can do precisely the same thing in any version of C by using the #define facility, but generally in a more laboured way.

6.12 FUNCTIONS

There are no routines in C, only functions. In other words, every call returns a value. The only exception to this is when the system permits you to define a function type void. Output operations generally produce only side-effects, so they are often performed by routines in other languages. In the C library they are functions. They generally return an error code if the operation cannot be performed. If it is successful, a conventional value such as zero or the input parameter is returned. Most input functions return the value input or, if this is not a scalar, a pointer to it.

A function name is immediately recognisable in C, because it must be followed by a round-bracketed set of arguments. Even if the function needs no arguments, the brackets must still be present to distinguish the name from that of a data item. This is so in both function definitions and function calls.

When a function is defined, the name must be preceded by a type specifier, unless the function returns a value of type int, when the type may be omitted. The types of the arguments must also be declared. The argument declarations are followed by the function body, which is a block consisting of the declarations and statements necessary for its evaluation. Thus we might declare

```
insert(n, p)
int n ;
struct node *p ;
{
function body
} ;
```

to be a general function for inserting an integer into a structure. A typical call might be simply

```
insert(573, next) ;
```

or, if the return value were to be treated as an indication of whether the function "worked" or not

```
if (insert(573, next)) . . . . ;
```

A function can return a pointer. For instance

```
char *strchr(s, c)
          char *s ;
          char c ;
```

might be the declarator for a function returning a pointer to the first appearance of a character c in a string s. Notice that the string is referred to through a pointer s. This is standard practice in C.

Functions in C may be defined only at the top level. This is in contrast to the practice in most other languages (including BCPL), where one function name may be local to the body of another function. The storage class of a function is thus normally extern. If the class is omitted, then this is what is presumed. Functions can also be declared static, when they are visible only in the module where they are defined. External functions, like external data items, are visible in any module where they have been referenced, and cannot be used in modules where they have not. The function references for a program are generally held in a header file and included when needed.

C requires only the specifications and the name in a subsequent reference.

```
extern float Bessel() ;
```

Since the parameters are not redeclared there is no check that parameter types match in calls of external functions. It is the programmer's job to ensure consistency. Most compilers will require you to include the storage specifier **extern** when redeclaring functions, and to omit it when giving the full definition. In this way a compiler can distinguish a reference from a definition.

6.13 PROGRAMS

A program in C is a sequence of function definitions and data declarations. Top level data declarations, i.e. declarations outside any function block, may be prefaced by the storage-class specifier **extern** or **static**; though if neither appears then **extern** is presumed. If the program is written in separately compiled modules, then only functions and (implicit or explicit) external data definitions can be made accessible in other modules.

One function must be named **main**. This defines the entry point when the program is executed. If the compiler allows, it can be declared type **void**; though it is often useful to make it return a status code after execution, which the operating system can make use of at the job-control level.

main can also have parameters, which provide a medium of communication between the job-control system and the user program. Most C compilers recognise at least two top-level variables, **argc** and **argv**. **argv** is an array of pointers to strings, and **argc** is an integer giving the count of them. **argc** and **argv** can be passed to the function **main** when it is entered. If this is desired, then the definition of **main** should start

```
main(argc, argv)
int argc;
char * argv[];
```

The strings pointed to by the elements of **argv** are arguments of the program call, in order as written. For instance, in UNIX, after the call

```
a.out −x somefile
```

argv[1] points to the string "−x", **argv[2]** (or **argv[argc]**) to "somefile", and argv[0] to "a.out". Other operating systems allow parameters to be passed similarly; but the details of the method may differ.

Arguments can be options controlling the mode of operation, file names, constants, or even job-control variables, in fact anything that the user may wish to pass to a program when he calls it. The program must contain code to interpret arguments in the desired manner.

Comments, which all good programmers scatter liberally throughout, start with /∗ and end with ∗/. A comment can appear anywhere that whitespace can appear; and it may extend over two or more lines. A common error is to terminate a comment with /∗ instead of ∗/.

6.14   THE PREPROCESSOR

So far we have said nothing about introducing *named* constants into C programs. This is because named constants are handled not by the compiler but by a simple macro preprocessor that comes into operation before the compiler proper. First, though, why do we want named constants? The reason is principally for readability. While most people can probably recognise the values of standard constants like pi and e when they see them, it is by no means clear that the integer 1 in a particular place in a program on colour graphics means "red", while 2 means "orange". The program would have been easier to understand if the words RED, ORANGE, and so on actually appeared. A second reason for named constants is shorthand, and hence accuracy. It is easier to write pi than 3.14159265358979.

The preprocessor searches the source text for lines starting with #. A line beginning with #define defines a macro; that is, it associates a name with a piece of text. No terminating semicolon is needed: the macro ends with the newline unless the latter has been escaped (usually with a backslash). After a macro has been defined, the preprocessor scans the rest of the source text looking for occurrences of the macro name, which it replaces with the defined text. Thus to achieve the replacement of RED by 1, ORANGE by 2, and so on, we write at the head of our program

```
#define RED 1
#define ORANGE 2
and so on.
```

Because it is a *pre*processor, it cannot interfere with the compiler; so we can use it to knock our own program text into a form suitable for the compiler. Thus, if you are accustomed to BCPL, you might like to

```
#define $( {
#define $) }
```

and stick with conventions you have become used to.

Later definitions using the same macro name replace earlier definitions. There is also a directive #undef that removes a macro definition, leaving the name either undefined or setting it back to an earlier value.

Thus #define − #undef pairs can be nested to a system-defined depth.

```
#define MAXINT 32767
#define MAXINT 65535
#undef MAXINT
```

returns MAXINT to the value 32767. Some C compilers have a facility for definition in the compile command. In UNIX you can provide definitions at the job-control level. The command cc calls the compiler. The command line

```
cc −DMAXINT=32767 program.c
```

has the same effect as if

```
#define MAXINT 32767
```

had appeared in file program.c

The C macro-preprocessor will accept macro arguments. For instance, having defined a general data-transfer function, we can create more specific macros as follows:

```
#define get(x) transfer(0, x)
#define put(x) transfer(1, x)
```

A macro call such as

```
get(V[j])
```

in the main body of the program would then be expanded to

```
transfer(0, V[j])
```

Several of the "functions" in the C run-time library are actually defined as macros calling more elementary functions, or simply as macros that expand into expressions. The chief difference between a macro and a genuine function is that one cannot have a pointer to the former.

A macro can have an arbitrary number of arguments up to a system-defined limit; but the number in the call must match the number in the definition. Actual arguments are simply copied; and they may take any form, except only that they may not contain commas, since commas are used as argument separators. However, arguments that are themselves expressions must be treated with caution, since operators outside the argument may have higher priority than operators within it, leading to an evaluation sequence different from what was intended. In general it is advisable to enclose formal arguments in parentheses if they are likely to be expanded into expressions. It is not always obvious when this is so, for when a macro has been expanded it is rescanned to search for other macros. This means that macros can appear as arguments of macros, and can even appear in the bodies of macros. It also means that macro expansion can lead to a non-terminating loop.

The preprocessor also introduces conditional compilation. Text between #if and #endif is compiled only when the (constant) expression following #if evaluates to "true", i.e. nonzero. There is also an #else form in which text between #if and #else is compiled if the expression is true, and that between #else and #endif if it is false. As an alternative to the simple #if directive, #ifdef followed by an identifier causes conditional compilation only if the identifier has previously been the subject of a #define directive not yet countermanded by an #undef, or if it has been defined by a −D option in the compile command.

C programs can be generated not only manually but also by the use of programming tools. This is particularly so under UNIX, where there are several program generators such as awk and yacc producing C programs. If there are errors, then the C compiler will print diagnostics. But the user will want these to refer not to lines of the generated program but to lines of the source code that he originally wrote, later processed by the program generator. The directive

    #line <constant> <filename>

"fools" the compiler into thinking, for the purpose of diagnosis, that it is compiling the named file, and is at the line given by the constant. Program generators are written so as to insert #line directives in appropriate places. The file name may be omitted. If this is done, then the default is the file name that was used by the previous #line directive.

Finally, the preprocessor enables text stored elsewhere to be included as if it were part of the current file. This is equivalent to the GET directive in BCPL and is particularly useful for incorporating "header" information containing external definitions, #-defined constants and macros. The directives

    #include "filename" and
    #include <filename>

cause the preprocessor to search various parts of the filestore for the named file and incorporate it for compilation. The way in which the two forms of the directive are handled is system-dependent. Under UNIX, quote marks cause the search to start in the directory of the file containing the #include directive, while angle brackets confine the search to standard library directories. #included files may themselves contain #include directives to a system-defined depth.

Chapter 7

C Expressions and Statements

C has a richer set of operators than any other widely used programming language with the exception of APL. The rules for precedence and associativity are quite complicated; but you will find that in practically every case C will do with an expression what you intended it to do. Highest in precedence are the *primary* operators. These are [], which denote array indices, (), which enclose function arguments or convert parts of expressions into primaries, and the union/structure selectors → and .. These all associate from left to right, so that chains of selectors such as

```
first.family→sibling→age
```

which we met in the last chapter, do what is expected.

7.1 UNARY OPERATORS

There is one unary (monadic) Boolean operator, !. Boolean quantities are represented by integers, zero being treated as false and any other value as true. ! performs Boolean inversion: it returns 1 as the result of !0; otherwise it returns 0. Bitwise logical inversion is a different operation, which is performed by ~. This converts *all* 0s into 1s and all 1s into 0s.

As well as the unary minus, there are two other unary arithmetic operators, ++ and −−. These increment and decrement an operand by unity, and so have a side-effect upon the operand itself. Placed before the operand they return the incremented (decremented) value: placed after, the value returned is that of the original operand. Thus

```
x = y++
```

assigns the current value of y to x and *then* increments it, while

```
x = ++y
```

assigns the incremented value. Notice that the use of ++ or −− itself implies an assignment, so the operand it is applied to must have a left value. It would make no sense to write, for instance, ++(p+q), though ++v[5] is quite legitimate.

The two addressing operators & and * also are unary. &, like ++ and
−− can only be applied to something that has a left value. In the last
chapter we gave two declarations

```
int *rblock[10];
int (*iblock)[10];
```

Since the operators [] have a higher binding power than *, the array
signature attaches itself immediately to rblock, defining it to be an array,
later specified to consist of pointers. In the second example, because ()
and [] associate from the left, the * attaches itself immediately to iblock,
which therefore becomes defined as a pointer to what is later defined as
an array of int.

We can extend the notation to declare even more complex array
structures. Thus

```
int (*ablock[5])[10] ;
```

defines ablock to be an array of 5 pointers to arrays of 10 integers, while

```
int (*(*pblock)[5])[10] ;
```

defines pblock as a pointer to an array of 5 pointers to arrays of 10
integers. It is important to get the distinctions between these declarations clear, because a similar convention is used in connection with
functions.

There are two further unary operators. One of these we shall leave
until we have considered the rules for handling mixed-mode arithmetic.
The other is the operator sizeof. It is not possible to tell, at least not
without diligent searching in the implementor's manual, and not always
even then, just how much space a compiler allots to a particular data
type, especially if it is a structure. But C is intended to be portable; and
there are operations that are sensitive to object size. The unary operator
sizeof takes as its operand either a variable name or a typename. In
either case, the operator returns an integer giving the size of the object
in bytes.

A *typename* is not quite the same thing as a type declarator. It could
be a simple name of a type, such as float, or the name tag attached to a
structure or union type. It could also be a complex declarator, but
without the declared identifier. Thus we could adapt the last declarator
given above as a typename to give the expression

```
sizeof int (*(*)[5])[10]
```

returning the size of the type "pointer to an array of 5 pointers to arrays of 10 integers". The string (*(*)[5])[10] is known as an *abstract delarator*.

All the unary operators have the same precedence, and associate from right to left. Take note however that associativity applies only to *adjacent* operators. If the operators are separated by operators of lower precedence, then the order of evaluation is undefined. For instance

a[i++] = b[i++]

will eventually cause double incrementation of i; but whether a or b gets the lower index depends on the implementation.

7.2 ARITHMETIC OPERATORS

Multiplicative operators have higher precedence than additive operators. There are three multiplicative operators: * for multiplication, / for division, and % for modular residue. The last may take only integer operands, and returns an integer result; thus the value of

45 % 7

is 3. If both operands are integers and both are positive, then division truncates towards zero, giving a positive remainder. If one integer operand is negative, then the quotient rounding, and hence the sign and value of the remainder, depends on the implementation.

The additive operators are + and −. Nothing more need be said about these, except that, as we have already noted, they are the only dyadic operators that may be applied to pointers. The relationship

pointer + integer = pointer

encompasses all that need be said about pointer arithmetic, and implies another legal relationship

pointer − pointer = integer

Pointer arithmetic of this sort is strictly meaningful only when the pointers apply to the same array. All arithmetic operators associate from left to right.

C permits mixed-mode arithmetic, that is, it permits the numeric types to be mixed in expressions. To make this possible, certain types must be converted, or *coerced* to other types before they are operated on. The rules may be summarised as follows:

All real arithmetic is performed in double precision.

Integer quantities are converted to double if they are mixed with real quantities.

Otherwise, if either operand is long, then the other is converted to long.

Otherwise, if either operand is unsigned, then the other is converted to unsigned.

Otherwise both operands are treated as int.

The result in each case is of the type of the operands.

A further coercion may occur when the result of evaluating an expression is assigned to a left-hand quantity. double is converted to float by rounding. It is converted to long or int by truncating the fractional part and dropping high-order bits if necessary. The conversion sequence long to int to short to char is achieved by dropping high-order bits, which may also have the effect of changing the sign. Conversion from short to int to long involves sign extension. That from char to short or int may or may not, according to the system.

When operands are passed to functions, float is coerced to double and char to int. There may be a further conversion, equivalent to that involved in assignment, when the function returns its result.

7.3 CASTS

Data typing is very valuable because it makes it possible for the compiler to detect many typical logical errors in programs. However, typing can sometimes be a bit restrictive. The C compiler will usually give a "type mismatch" diagnostic if you try to pass an argument of one type to a function that is expecting another type, or if you try to use a pointer to one type of object as a pointer to another type, even though such operations might seem quite unexceptionable. One way to avoid the first difficulty would be to assign the variable first to a variable of an appropriate type, relying on the normal coercion effect, and pass this latter to the function. The second problem, though, is not so easy to solve. You can solve both problems quite simply though in C by using a *cast*.

The cast operator is the last unary operator, which we deferred discussing before. It consists simply of a typename in parentheses, and serves to coerce the operand directly to the type given. Thus we might write a command of the form

```
printf("/N%d     %f", j, sin((double)j)) ;
```

in which an integer j is passed as a double-precision number to the real function sin. We have already discussed typenames in connection with sizeof operator, and we have seen that they can be quite complex, particularly in relation to pointers. Casting is legitimate for any of the arithmetic conversions that can occur in expressions. In addition, any pointer can be cast to a pointer to char. Although in theory any pointer can be cast to any other pointer, this cannot always be guaranteed owing to the problem of alignment in memories more than one byte wide. However, all the memory-allocation functions in the standard library (see the next chapter) should be guaranteed to accept any reasonable cast.

7.4 BITWISE OPERATORS

C has a number of operators that handle integer types as sequences of bits. Highest in precedence among these are the shift operators >> and << . They return the bit pattern of the first operand shifted by the number of places given by the second operand. The vacant places in either sense of shift are filled with zeros; and bits shifted off are lost. The effect (except for the lost bits) is the same as multiplication or unsigned integer division by a power of 2. Thus

        12 << 3 yields 96
and   26 >> 2 yields 6

The shift operators have precedence immediately below the addition operators, and associate from left to right.

The dyadic bitwise logical operators are, in descending order of precedence, & (AND), ∧ (XOR) and | (OR). They are all commutative; and their effects on individual bit pairs is given in the following table:

		&	∧	|
0	0	0	0	0
0	1	0	1	1
1	1	1	0	1

7.5 RELATIONS

The relational operators operate on pairs of integers to yield an integer result that is either zero (false) or unity (true). There are four ordering relations: >, <, >=, <=. These all have higher priority than the equality and inequality relations, respectively == and !=. Notice the double "equals" symbol. Using = in mistake for == is a common error among inexperienced C programmers.

The precedence level of the relational operators as a whole is between that of the shift operators and that of the bitwise logicals. They all associate from left to right. There is no extended relation as there is in BCPL.

a > b > c means (a > b) > c

i.e. it tests whether 0 or 1, according to the truth of a > b, exceeds c. Relational operators may be applied to pointers as well as integers; though, strictly speaking, the result is meaningful only if the two operands point to the same array.

7.6 BOOLEANS

Boolean operators, in contrast to bitwise operators, treat the whole operand as a single logical value, false if zero, true if nonzero. There are two dyadic Boolean operators. In order of precedence they are && and ||. In the full scale of precedence they come below the bitwise logical operators, and hence below the relationals. Consequently expressions such as

a > b && c < d

evaluate in the natural way without parentheses. Boolean operators associate from left to right.

7.7 CONDITIONAL EXPRESSIONS

The form of a conditional expression in C is

a ? b : c

where a is treated as a Boolean value and b and c can be any type of expression. a is evaluated first. If it yields the value "true", then b is evaluated to give the value of the expression: if not, then the value of the expression is that of c. If b and c are of different types, then type conversions occur in the manner already discussed; consequently the type of the result is independent of the truth of the precedent expression. The precedence is below that of the Booleans. However, only one of b and c is evaluated; so a side effect such as ++x in either b or c may or may not occur. Associativity is from right to left, so that expressions can be nested without the need for brackets.

7.8 ASSIGNMENT OPERATORS

Assignment in C is treated as an expression, and can form part of a larger expression, producing a side-effect when the expression is evaluated. The simple assignment operator is = ; but assignment can be combined with any of the dyadic arithmetic or bitwise operators as a convenient shorthand notation. Thus

    a += b

is the same as

    a = a + b

except in one important respect. a, if it is an expression, is evaluated only once.

The other assignment operators are −=, *=, /=, %=, >>=, <<=, &=, ∧= and |=. Since add operators can combine integers and pointers, += and −= can take a pointer on the left-hand side and an integer on the right. In the other cases, both operands must be of a type that would be appropriate to the operator. A pointer may be assigned to an integer or an integer to a pointer; but, except in the case when zero (null) is assigned, the result is system-dependent.

The value of an expression containing an assignment operator is the same as the final value of the left-hand side. Assignments have a lower precedence than any of the operators so far considered; so both sides must be fully evaluated before the assignment and any operation associated with it can take place. Assignment operators associate from right to left; so

    x += y += 3

assigns y+3 to y and x+y+3 to x.

7.9 THE COMMA OPERATOR

In the expression

    a , b

where a and b may be expressions of any type, the effect is to evaluate both a and b in that order and return the value of b as the value of the expression. Obviously such an expression is purposeless unless a has a side effect. A common application for the expression before the comma operator is to initialise one or more variables for local use in the expression after. In this it can be compared with the WHERE conjunction in CPL. Thus (a,b) may be regarded as equivalent to b WHERE a in which a binds free variables for use by b.

It is important to make a clear distinction between the comma when used as an operator and the same symbol when used as a separator. If there is any danger of confusion, then the expression using the comma operator must be placed in parentheses, e.g.

    f(x, (y++, ++y−2))

which passes the original value of y as its second argument to the function f, but leaves y increased by 2. The comma has the lowest precedence of all the operators. It associates from left to right.

Here in summary is a list of all the operators used in C in order of precedence, together with their associativity.

() [] −> .	l − r
! ~ ++ −− − (type) * & sizeof	r − l
* / %	l − r
+ −	l − r
<< >>	l − r
< <= > >=	l − r
== !=	l − r
&	l − r
^	l − r
|	l − r
&&	l − r
||	l − r
?:	r − l
= += −= etc.	r − l
,	l − r

7.10 SIMPLE STATEMENTS

Any C expression can be used as a statement simply by terminating it with a semicolon. The effect is to evaluate the expression (with all its side−effects) and discard the result. Thus

    x = y ; a += 3 ; p++ ; f(z) ;

are expressions that can be used meaningfully as statements, since all have, or can have, side-effects. The coincidence between statements and expressions in C, properly made use of, can lead to appreciable savings in both source and object code.

A null statement, ; , is permissible. It is useful for the "do nothing while ..." sort of construction, and for carrying a label. A label can preced any statement, and is an identifier followed by a colon. It may be used only in connection with the goto statement. This takes the form

```
goto label ;
```

and should ideally not be used at all. C does not permit pointers to labels, though the switch statement can be used to provide, within the limitations of the system, an equivalent facility. Because label identifiers can be used only with goto, most compilers will allow them to be overloaded copies of identifiers used in other contexts.

7.11 BLOCKS

A sequence of statements may be enclosed between braces, when they are together called a *block*. Optionally the statements in a block may be preceded by one or more declarations. These create automatic names unless another storage class is expressly stated. A block is syntactically equivalent to a single statement, and has no need itself of a terminating semicolon, though there must still be a semicolon to terminate the last statement in a block, in contrast to the practice in some other languages.

7.12 FUNCTIONS

A function is a named and (optionally) parameterised expression. The statement

```
return expression ;
```

is the normal way to define the value of a function and return control to the point of call. The expression is converted, if necessary, to the type of the function, and is substituted for the function name in the call. If there is no return statement, control is returned when it reaches the end of the function body. The returned value is then undetermined. This may be quite legitimate if the function call is a statement, i.e. if it stands alone terminated by a semicolon, or if it forms the first part of a comma expression. The return statement need carry no expression, when the returned value is likewise undetermined.

The arguments in a function call are passed *by value* in C; that is to say, they are evaluated at call time, and the results (effectively) substituted for the formal parameters in the function definition. Arguments may of course be pointers, in which case the indirect value (contents) of the argument is passed *by reference*. Assignment to an indirect argument passed in this way changes the value of the original parameter. Readers familiar with Pascal will find a parallel between pointer parameters in C and var parameters in Pascal. Arrays, as we have seen, are represented by pointers; so array parameters too are passed by reference.

In C, functions can return pointers as well as accept them as arguments. Not only this, but they can themselves be referred to by pointers. If we declare

    float (*Poisson)(x)

we declare the name Poisson to be, not the *name* of a function that returns a value of type float, but a pointer to such a function. Having defined a pointer to a function, we can manipulate it in the same way that we can manipulate any other pointer. For instance, we can assign it to a new (pointer) variable

    p = Poisson

and call it under its new name.

    y = (*p)(t)

Notice the need for bracketing the *p. This is because (t) has a higher binding power than *.

Sometimes it is necessary to pass a function as an argument to another function. Suppose for instance that we wished to write a general integral function that would integrate any continuous function beween given limits. We might declare such a function as follows:

    float integral(fp, llim, ulim)
            float llim, ulim, (*fp)() ;
    {
    . . . . . .
    }

fp is then defined as a pointer to a function; and any reference to it in the function body would have to be of a form such as

    (*fp)(llim + n*h)

(The second * here is the multiply operator.)

In any call of integral, the first parameter must be a pointer to a function. This could be provided explicitly; but C permits pointers to functions to be passed by implication; i.e. it would permit in this case a function call of the form

    integral(g, −1, 1) ;

g here carries no parentheses. The C compiler interprets this as an instruction not to evaluate g at a particular abscissa but merely to pass a pointer to it as the parameter instead. Passing a function as a parameter of course is quite different from passing an argument that is the *result* of applying the function at a particular abscissa, e.g.

    y = f(g(x))

Notice that there is no way that the compiler can check that g is compatible with the way formal parameter fp is used within the body of integral. In this case g would have to be a real function taking a single real parameter. The absence of a compiler check is generally regarded as a weakness in C, since it allows logical errors to creep in that cannot be detected until execution. However, there are usually additional constraints upon parameters, particularly those of mathematical functions, that can in no way be detected by a compiler. In this case, for instance, the function would have to be continuous between the limits of integration.

As with arrays, we can write very complex function structures if we wish. For instance,

    float (*fp())()

declares fp to be a function that returns a pointer to a function of type float, and

    float *(*fblock())[]

declares fblock as a function returning a pointer to an array of pointers to floating-point numbers. The meaning of a particular complex declaration can be determined by carefully considering the relative precedence of the operators used.

7.13 CONDITIONAL STATEMENTS

A conditional statement in C takes the form

    if (expression) statement

or

if (expression) statement **else** statement

In the first form, the statement is executed only if the bracketed expression evaluates to nonzero (true). In the second form, the first statement is executed if the expression is true: the second if it is false. Remember that a C statement is terminated by a semicolon; so, unless the statement controlled by if is a block, a semicolon should appear just before else.

7.14 INDEFINITE LOOPS

The simplest form of indefinite loop is

while (expression) statement

The statement is executed repeatedly so long as the expression evaluates to "true". The other form of indefinite loop is

do statement while (expression) ;

In this case the statement is executed at least once. Subsequent execution cycles depend on the value of the expression.

If the loop controls a single statement rather than a block, then a semicolon should appear in front of the while in a do loop. In general though, the while statement will control a block. It is possible to exit from the block part way through by using the statement break ;, which will usually be controlled by an if. break takes control to the next statement following the loop. A common idiom is a continuous loop from which the only escape is a break statement.

```
while (1) {
        . . . . . .
      if (....) break ;
        . . . . . .
      }
```

You can also omit part of a loop by using continue;, which takes control direct to the next while test. goto can also be used to jump within or out of a loop; and the return statement will by implication also take control out of a loop.

Because assignment is treated in C as an expression, it is perfectly legitimate to write a statement like

while (x = y) ....;

The condition in this case is true if the assignment expression returns nonzero, that is, if y is nonzero. It is thus independent of the original value of x; and it has a side effect. Its operation is thus quite different from

```
while (x == y) ........;
```

which simply tests for equality between x and y, and may have been what was meant in the first place. *Confusing = with == is perhaps the single most common cause of error among inexperienced programmers in C.* Nevertheless the first form is often useful, and can lead to more concise programming. For instance, the statement

```
while (*s++ = *t++) ;
```

following suitable declarations for s and t can be used to transfer successive data items from one array to another until a zero item is encountered.

7.15 COUNTING LOOPS

Because of side effects in expressions, you can always write a concise counting loop using while alone,

```
while (j++ < limit) .... ;
```

for instance. Nevertheless, for users who are accustomed to a more conventional syntax, C provides the structure

```
for (e1; e2; e3) statement
```

The idea is that expression e1 is executed once, before entry to the loop, e3 is executed repetitively immediately after the controlled statement, which is executed so long as e2 is true. Thus the for statement is equivalent to

```
e1;
while (e2) {
statement
e3;
}
```

break and continue can be used to exit from the loop. continue transfers control to a point just before e3 is evaluated. break takes control to a point just after the closing brace.

A conventional counting loop might appear as

    for (j=0; j<limit; j++) . . . ;

But notice that j must have been declared already outside the loop, in contrast to BCPL in which the control variable is declared automatically. Also in contrast to BCPL the limit can be changed *from within* the loop by replacing limit with a variable expression.

Since the test for e2 is made *before* each repetition of the controlled statement, there is no execution when j == limit, though j does eventually take up that value. Any of the three expressions may be omitted. If the second is omitted, then the condition is taken to be identically "true". A continuous loop, terminable only with a break, can be written as

    for (; ;) . . . . ;

though it could as well be written

    while (1) . . . . ;

7.16 SWITCHES

The normal form of the switch statement in C is

    switch (expression) block

where certain statements within the block carry label prefixes of the form

    case constant expression :

Notice that a *constant* expression is required so that the tests can be compiled without interpretive features. The expressions should be of the same type as the expression following the switch keyword. Pointer and floating-point types are not permitted. Two or more prefixes may be applied to the same statement, though they must then have constant expressions of different value. One prefix may be of the form

    default :

The variable expression at the start of the switch statement is evaluated; and the result is compared in turn with the values of the constant expressions in the case labels. If a match is found, then control jumps immediately to that point. If not, control jumps to the default label if there is one; otherwise the whole of the controlled block is skipped. The statement break ; is normally used to force exit from a switch block after the statement or statements following a case label have been executed. In the absence of a break statement, control passes unimpeded across label prefixes.

It is worth noting that the syntax defines a switch statement as

switch (expression) statement

In short, the switch does not have to control a block. The result is that many compilers will allow you to use case in bizarre ways — to jump to a selection of entry points within a while loop, for instance. Constructions like this should be avoided.

Chapter 8

The C Library

C systems provide a range of precompiled functions and macros that users can incorporate in their own programs. The macros are in header files. The functions can be found in any of three places:

> predeclared in the compiler itself,
> in the standard C library,
> in other libraries.

Predeclared functions are automatically incorporated during compliation; and you need not take any special action to include them. Functions in the standard library are incorporated during the linker pass after compilation. However, they are external, so must be redeclared in every module where they are used. This is best done using the appropriate header file.

The directive

```
#include <stdio.h>
```

appearing at the start of a module incorporates a header file that causes all references to functions in the standard input and output library to be treated as external. It also includes several input and output macros. The angle brackets ensure that the search for stdio.h starts at a standard place (in UNIX, the directory /usr/include). In UNIX the library is automatically incorporated by the compile command cc. If the command ld is used to perform the linking, then −lc must be typed at the end of the list of modules to be linked.

Libraries other than the standard must be incorporated explicitly. In UNIX writing −lx at the end of the list of modules in a compile command causes selections from the library /lib/libx.a or /usr/lib/libx.a to be linked into the final object code. A header file redeclaring the library functions must also be included in all modules that make use of them.

The standard library provides a defined type called FILE. In fact this is a structure giving in a system-dependent manner the parameters necessary to describe a device or file together with the instantaneous status of its associated buffer. Most operations on files use pointers to these structures – sometimes referred to as *streams*. There are three predeclared streams: stdin, stdout and stderr. The first of these is initially assigned to the keyboard, and the other two to the CRT screen.

8.1 KEYBOARD INPUT AND SCREEN OUTPUT

The simplest input and output functions are getchar() and putchar(c), which operate respectively on stdin and stdout. In fact they are not functions but macros in stdio.h, which expand into calls to system functions. In practice, the only significant difference between a true function and a macro is that one cannot create a pointer to the latter, so cannot pass it as a parameter.

getchar() returns the next character in stdin. It returns the standard EOF symbol when it reaches the end of a file. This is defined in stdio.h, and normally has the value -1; but you should use EOF rather than -1 to ensure portability. putchar(c) outputs character c to stdout. It returns the character just output, or EOF in case of error.

8.2 FILES

The structures of type FILE are organised as an array, whose (installation dependent) dimension limits the number of files that can be associated with one program. stdin, stdout and stderr normally point to elements 0, 1 and 2 of this array. Other streams are created by first declaring a new file pointer, e.g.

    FILE * fp

and then *opening* an actual file or device in association with it. This can be done by a call to the library function fopen, which initialises the next structure in the array of FILE, and returns a pointer to it. So we can assign a value to the pointer fp by using a statement such as

    fp = fopen(filename, mode) ;

filename must be a string (constant or variable); but the form of string that is permissible is system-dependent. In UNIX it is any allowable pathname. fopen does not normally allocate a buffer. This is done by the first call to a read or write function on the stream, which goes through the same motions as it does after it empties a buffer (on reading) or fills one to capacity (on writing).

The mode too is a string, usually of one character. Allowable modes are:

> "r" open an existing file for reading, position at start,
> "w" create a new file, or clear an existing one, for writing or
>   overwriting,
> "a" open to append, position at end.

It is illegal to read from files opened in modes "w" or "a", or to write to files opened in mode "r". A + after the mode letter generally legalises such operations, though it is often necessary to reposition files first.

fopen positions the file at either end, depending on the mode. A function rewind (fp) will position the file pointed to by fp at its start whatever was its previous position. It is possible to position a file at any arbitrary point by using the function

    fseek(fp, offset, from)

The file designated by fp is then positioned the number of bytes given by offset from the position indicated by from. Because of the length of a typical file, offset should be a long integer, which, if the file comprises anything but a simple sequence of characters, may be calculated with the aid of sizeof. The value of from is normally zero, indicating that offset is to be counted from the beginning of the file. Values 1 and 2 enable the offset to be computed from from the current position or from the end respectively. rewind(fp) is therefore equivalent to fseek(fp, 0L, 0). There is also a function ftell(fp), which returns a long integer giving the current position of the file from its start.

    fseek(fp, ftell(fp), 0)

thus leaves a file where it was.

The presence of an "open" function predicates that of a "close" function to release the file or device for use by other processes. fclose(fp) takes as its parameter the file pointer returned by fopen, and returns zero if the file can be closed successfully, otherwise it returns EOF. fclose should flush an associated output buffer, sending any characters still in it to the output device. You can use the function fflush(fp) if you want to empty the buffer but still keep the channel open.

There is also a useful function

    freopen(filename, mode, fp)

This first closes any stream associated with the file pointer fp, and then opens a new file in the specified mode, associating it with the same pointer fp, which it returns, provided naturally that the operation can be performed. If not, it returns EOF. Thus the use of freopen ensures continuity in the use of a particular file pointer.

Several systems permit standard input and standard output to be redirected when the program is loaded. In UNIX

    < sourcename

written after a command to run a program causes the file or device referred to as "sourcename" to be opened during the program set-up phase and associated with the pointer stdin. Similarly

> destination

causes the file or device "destination" to be opened and associated with stdout. Functions getchar and putchar then operate on the new source and destination. The same effect can be achieved during execution by using freopen.

If more than one input or output stream is open at the same time, you can use

getc(fp) and putc(c, fp)

which allow you to specify the data stream on each call. Because putc and getc are macros not functions, most libraries provide true functions fputc and fgetc as well. True functions occupy less space *in toto* if several calls appear in the program text; but they operate more slowly than the equivalent macros because of the overhead imposed by transferring control. getc, like getchar returns the next character in the selected input stream, and putc, like putchar returns the character written or EOF. getchar() and putchar(c) are therefore the same as getc(stdin) and putc(c, stdout).

There is also a function (not a macro)

ungetc(c, fp)

which pushes c back on to the designated stream, so that it will be reread by the next getc. ungetc must be used intelligently. You cannot unget what you have not yet got; and you cannot push EOF back into an input stream.

Though files are normally accessed through pointers, a file may alternatively be referred to by a small integer, sometimes known as a *handle*. In most implementations the handle in fact is the file's index in the array of FILE; so the handles of stdin, stdout and stderr are likely to be 0, 1 and 2 respectively. There is a set of low-level functions that use file handles in place of stream pointers.

The function

open(filename, mode)

creates a new FILE entry in the array, associates it with the given file name, and returns the integer handle. open operates like fopen. It will normally work only if the file already exists. It cannot create a new file;

though in some implementations there are opening modes to do this. In others a separate function creat is needed. There is also a corresponding function

close(handle)

which operates like fclose.

Low-level input and output are performed by the functions

read(handle, buffer, length)

and

write(handle, buffer, length)

buffer should be an array of char of size length, which in turn should be an integral multiple of the sector length for a block-type device. These functions may be called by the higher level getc and putc to replenish the buffer when it empties or flush it when full. You can get some idea of the input-output mechanism used by a particular implementation by studying stdio.h.

8.3 STRINGS

The functions

puts(str) and gets(buf)

provide for simple string output and input respectively. str is a pointer to char; and characters are written to stdout up to, but not including, the null string terminator. They are followed by a newline. puts is an integer function, which returns EOF in case of error; otherwise the returned value is unspecified. gets reads characters up to the next newline. buf is a character array, whose declaration should have made it long enough to accommodate any likely input string. The newline is not stored, but is replaced by a string terminator. gets returns a null pointer in case of error; otherwise it returns its argument.

puts and gets

operate on standard input and output.

fputs(str, fp) and fgets(buf, n, fp)

give access to arbitrary channels. fputs operates just like puts; but fgets allows a limit count n to be specified. It is thus safer than gets, since the buffer can be protected from overflow. It differs further from gets in that a newline is stored (followed by a terminator) if one is read before the count runs out. Like gets, fgets returns either a null pointer or its first argument.

8.4   UNFORMATTED INPUT AND OUTPUT

The function

    fread(bp, size, count, fp)

reads a binary block from the stream designated by fp into a buffer pointed to by bp. The data is presumed to comprise a sequence of items whose size is given by the size parameter (generally computed by the sizeof operator). count gives the maximum number of items to be read: the function returns the actual number. The two of course are the same unless end-of-file intervenes. It is important to appreciate that fread is essentially a string-read function. It cannot generally be used to read and store a record structure in the manner of a READ statement in COBOL.

The function

    fwrite(bp, size, count, fp)

performs the converse operation. It returns the number of items written, unless an error occurs, when it returns zero.

8.5   FORMATTED OUTPUT

The function

    printf(format string, item list) ;

provides within the scope of a single function a wide variety of output facilities. The format string can be simply a sequence of characters to be output, e.g.

    printf("end of run/n") ;

the /n forcing a newline. If there are variables to be printed, then each must have its appropriate control code embedded in the format string and signalled by a % symbol. The identifiers of the variables to be output then follow in the same order as their control codes. Thus, for instance, the call

    printf("name %s status /"%c/" age %d/n", name, marital, age) ;

might produce the output line

name James Jones status "m" age 45

the first two backslashes being used to force two quote symbols to be printed.

Each format control symbol consists of the % sign followed by any or all of the following, only the last being mandatory:

a flag: − to left justify,

+ to insert a sign

0 for zero insertion

a decimal numeric indication of the field width,

a stop, followed by the precision, giving the number of significant characters to be output,

an I or L to indicate long,

the control character.

You can include a quoted % in the format string as %%. If the field width is omitted, the number of characters will be the minimum necessary. The control characters used are:

d	signed decimal conversion
u	unsigned decimal
o	unsigned octal
x	unsigned hexadecimal with no leading zero unless requested
c	single character
s	string, truncated if longer than precision
e	float or double in the form (−)m.pppppppE(+/−)cc, where the number of p's is given by the precision (default 6)
f	float or double in the form (−)mmm.pppppp, where the number of p's is determined by the precision and the maximum number of m's by this and the width
g	whichever is shorter of e or f.

These rules are a bit complicated, and they do differ a little from implementation to implementation. The best way is to experiment until you get the layout you want. There are close similarities with FOR-TRAN conventions for those who are familiar with them.

printf sends output to the current standard output channel. There is a function

fprintf(fp, format string, item list)

that works similarly but allows you to select an arbitrary output channel fp. Some systems provide a function putw(i,fp) for integer output. If yours does not, and you have substantial integer output, you can create a macro

```
#define putw(i,fp) fprintf(fp,"%d ",i)
```

to do the same job.

There is also a function

sprintf(**string**, format, item list)

which enables you to format output items but transfer them not to an output device but to the designated string in memory. The three functions discussed in this section are all integer functions. They return the number of characters printed, except in case of error, when -1 is returned.

8.6   FORMATTED INPUT

The function

scanf(format string, pointer list)

reads items from the standard input, converts them according to the format provided, and assigns values in turn to the items listed. Notice that items must be passed as *pointers* to scanf, otherwise their values cannot be altered. C provides complex facilities for formatted input that were devised in the era of the punched card; though most users' needs now are more modest.

The format control symbols consist of a % character and a conversion code. Between these, optionally, may appear:

an assignment-suppression (ignore) flag, *,

maximum field width in decimal,

a size specification, h for short, l for long, giving the magnitude of the converted quantity.

The conversion codes recognised by scanf are

d	decimal integer
u	unsigned decimal integer
o	octal integer
x	hexadecimal integer
h	short (decimal) integer
c	single character

s   string delimited by whitespace (the function adds a ter-
        minal /0 in memory)

e or f floating-point number in either %e or %f format (see
        above).

[]   scan input searching for characters enclosed, and assign
        these as a string to the next pointer.

Whitespace between format items is ignored. If any characters other than whitespace appear in the format string but are not preceded by %, then they must match characters in the corresponding position in the input. Whitespace in the input is treated as a field separator unless a field width is specified; otherwise it is ignored.

There is a function

    fscanf(fp, format, pointer list)

to provide for formatted input from an arbitrary data stream fp. There is also a formatted string-read function for in-memory conversion

    sscanf(string, format, pointer list)

These both operate in a similar way to scanf. All three functions return EOF if the scan cannot be completed; otherwise they return the number of successfully converted input items. Because of this it is not easy to devise a macro equivalent to the simple decimal input function getw(fp), which is provided in some systems. The closest is to use the comma operator, thus

    #define getw(fp) (fscanf(fp,"%d ",p) , *p)

but the pointer p has to be declared somewhere in the program.

8.7   STRING CONVERSION

Input in C makes use of conversion functions that may themselves be available in the library. The function atoi(str) converts the string indicated by str into an integer, which it returns. Conversion ends with the first non-convertible character in the string. A function atol(str) may also be available for converting strings to long integers. We shall discuss floating-point conversion later when we consider the mathematical library.

8.8 BOOLEANS

The I/O library provides several useful test functions. feof(fp) is a macro that returns "true" if the end of the file pointed to by fp has been reached, "false" otherwise. It is particularly useful in connection with those functions for which EOF is a permissible returned value, and therefore ambiguous. ferror(fp) tests whether an error has occurred on a transfer to or from the channel associated with fp. The value returned is a system-dependent error code. Do not make the mistake of assuming that the error is automatically reset when the file is interrogated. clearerr(fp) must be used for this.

8.9 CHARACTER PROCESSING

The standard facilities include a set of test and conversion macros for handling characters. They can be made available through a header file ctype.h. The test macros are listed below. We give their definitions as if the internal code were ASCII; but they should work correctly even if not.

Function	True if character is in
isalpha(c)	a – z, A – Z
isalnum(c)	0 – 9, a – z, A – Z
isascii(c)	ASCII codes 0 – 127
iscntrl(c)	ASCII codes 0 – 31
isprint(c)	ASCII codes 32 – 127
isdigit(c)	0 – 9
islower(c)	a – z
isupper(c)	A – Z
isspace(c)	whitespace
ispunct(c)	ASCII codes 33 – 47, 58 – 64, 91 – 95, 123 – 127

To go with these tests, file ctype.h provides conversion macros toupper(c) and tolower(c), which convert the case of alphabetic characters. There is also a macro toint(c), which converts A to F and a to f into their hexadecimal integer "weights", 10 to 15. Characters 0 to 9 are returned unchanged by toint; and any other character returns −1. Finally, for those systems that do not employ ASCII internally, toascii(c) should convert the system's own representation to the standard code for the character given in c.

8.10 MATHEMATICAL FUNCTIONS

The standard library provides a few integer functions, which can be made use of without taking special measures. These include abs(n), which accepts only in-range integers, and the long-integer function labs(L). There is also rand(), which provides on successive calls a sequence of pseudorandom integers in the range 0 to the maximum value of int. The seed for the sequence is 1 by default; but another seed can be sown by the function srand(seed), where seed is an *unsigned* value.

The mathematical library is separate from the standard library, and must usually be linked separately to the object program. In UNIX this is done by including −lm at the end of the command to compile or link. It is also necessary to quote the directive

```
#include <math.h>
```

in every module that makes use of this library. math.h not only redeclares all the functions in the library, it also defines a system-dependent value HUGE, which is the largest double-precision number that can be handled. All the functions return a value of type double, even those that return an integral quantity, like floor(x) and ceil(x), which respectively return the next integer below, and the next integer above, x.

The mathematical library includes the usual circular, hyperbolic, and logarithmic functions:

```
acos(x), asin(x), atan(x), atan2(x,y), cos(x),
cosh(x), exp(x), hypot(x,y), log(x), log10(x),
sin(x), sinh(x), tan(x), tanh(x).
```

atan2 uses the signs of both coordinates to determine the quadrant: acos yields a value between 0 and pi, while the other circular functions give values between −pi/2 and pi/2. hypot computes sqrt(x∗x + y∗y). The library also includes a function sqrt(x) as well as pow(x, y) (needed because there is no exponentiation operator in C) and a real absolute function fabs(x). There is also a conversion function atof(s), which converts a string s in either floating-point format into a value of type double.

Other functions in the mathematical library are concerned with scaling floating-point numbers. modf(x, np) (also known as fmod(x, np)) returns the fractional part of a double-precision number x, and places its integer part in the location pointed to by np. For numbers whose range.

is too large for this to be done, frexp(x, np) returns a mantissa less than 1.0, and places in the location denoted by np an exponent such that multiplying the mantissa by a system-dependent base, usually 2, raised to the exponent power would reconstitute the original number. The converse of this is ldexp(m, n), which returns a double precision number giving the product of the mantissa m by the base raised to the power n.

8.11 PROCESSING STRINGS

The standard library contains several functions for handling strings. These are accessible in modules carrying the appropriate header, either <string.h> or <strings.h>. They provide facilities for copying and catenating strings, for comparing them, and for finding the first occurrence of a particular character in them. When these functions are used in such a way as to alter the length of a string, it is important for the original declaration to have given a size sufficient for any length of string that may have to be accommodated. If this is not done, memory beyond the end of the string may get corrupted.

strcpy(s, t), where s and t are character pointers, replaces string s with a copy of string t, and returns the pointer s. strcat(s, t) attaches string t to the end of string s, overwriting the original null terminator of s. The pointer s is returned. If the two strings overlap in memory, the result is undefined.

An integer function strcmp(s, t) compares two strings lexicographically, returning a negative value if s is less than t, a positive value if s is greater than t, and zero if the two are identical. A string is lexicographically less than another if at the first character position in which they differ the character in the first has a lower code than the character in the second. If the two strings match up to the end of one, then the shorter string is lexicographically less than the longer.

It is sometimes necessary to search strings for particular patterns. The function index(s, c) (alias strchr(s, c)) returns a pointer to the first occurrence of character c in string s. If the search fails, the NULL pointer is returned. Remember that the argument s does not have to point to the beginning of the string; so you can search for successive occurrences of c by using the pointer returned by one search as the argument s for the next. You can find the end of the string by searching '/0'. index searches forwards. A function rindex(s, c) (strrchr(s, c)) searches backwards from s. Another, strpos(s, c), provided in some implementations, is similar to index, except that it is an integer function returning the character's position instead of a pointer to it.

The foregoing functions more than cover the full set in the Kernighan-Ritchie "standard". Most implementations provide additions. With a view to avoiding the chaos that usually follows if the end of a string is overflowed, functions strncpy(s, t, n) and strncat(s, t, n) operate like strcpy and strcat, but move at most n characters. If fewer than n characters are available to move, then the result is padded out with nulls. There is also a function strncmp(s, t, n) in which at most n characters are compared. An integer function strlen(s) returns the length of string s, up to, but not including, the null terminator; and this can be used to determine the third parameter. An alias lenstr appears in some implementations.

Various other string functions are provided in individual implementations. There are for instance functions that search not for a single character but for one among a specified set of characters. These are best studied by consulting the particular implementation manual.

8.12 STORAGE ALLOCATION

Something that C provides that is seldom offered in other programming languages is the ability to request additional memory during execution. This, together with the ability to free memory again, saves the user from having to guess the storage needs of a program, and can lead to efficient memory use if the needs change during execution. It is particularly useful if a program is generated, not produced manually.

In the Kernighan-Ritchie "standard" there is just one allocation function

```
calloc(n, size)
```

This allocates enough contiguous memory to accommodate n items of length size, sets the whole region to zero, and returns a character pointer to the start of it. It returns a null pointer if sufficient memory cannot be found. The argument size is typically generated by applying the sizeof operator to a suitable typename. If the resulting memory block is to be used as an array, then a cast should be used to convert the pointer to a pointer of the appropriate type. A typical call of calloc might therefore be

```
ptr = ( P ) calloc( boxful, sizeof(P)) ;
```

The maximum quantity of memory that can be allocated by calloc is limited by the maximum value of argument n, which is of type int. This may not be enough for certain system applications. Some implementations therefore provide an alternative function clalloc(L, size) where the element count, L, is of type long. The size of the memory block is stored in a descriptor so that it can be released subsequently for possible reuse. The function cfree(ptr) will release a previously allocated block provided that ptr was obtained in the first place by the use of calloc or clalloc.

A more general allocation function in some implementations is

   malloc(size)

where size is the number of bytes in any type of object — an array, say. Memory allocated by malloc is not initialised to zero; and is freed by the function free(ptr), where ptr was returned by a previous malloc. There may also be a function mlalloc(size), where size is of type long. realloc(ptr, size) can be used to change the size of an allocated block (designated by ptr) while retaining its contents. It returns a pointer to the modified block, which may have been moved in memory.

The function alloca(size) does not, like the preceding functions, normally claim additional space from the operating system. Instead it allocates space on the stack, returning a pointer to it. Such space is automatically freed on exit from the current block. The function can therefore be used to create arrays whose storage class is truly automatic, and which can therefore be referred to recursively. The facility is particularly useful for creating search trees in artificial-intelligence applications.

The foregoing functions are held in the standard library; but it may be necessary to use a header file malloc.h to make them accessible externally. They can be uneconomic when a lot of small pieces of memory are requested, so some implementations provide extra allocation functions at a lower level and oriented to particular architectures.

8.13 EXCEPTION PROCESSING

Some implementations of C provide a longjump facility similar to that provided by BCPL. This is useful for processing exceptions — unusual events due sometimes to data errors, at others to faults on peripheral devices. A long jump takes control direct from an inner block to one enclosing it, by implication bypassing unexecuted code in intermediate blocks.

A typical scheme, which parallels that provided in BCPL, is to provide a setjump function in the block that is to be the destination of the long jump. The code for using this might be as follows:

```
ret.val = setjump(save);
if (ret.val == 0)
            { code for normal processing }
else
            { code for exceptions }
```

save is a buffer that will contain data defining the stack height at the time and the location of the next instruction after setjump. setjump returns zero; so after setting the appropriate values in save it proceeds to execute the code for normal processing.

The inner block should then contain code such as

```
if error longjump(save, err.no)
```

This restores the stack to a condition stored in the buffer save, and transfers control to a point just after the setjump that defined the contents of save. It also returns err.no as if it had been returned by setjump, i.e. it assigns its value to ret.val. If this is nonzero, the code for exceptions is then executed, err.no being available if necessary to switch to the appropriate action.

Chapter 9

C and UNIX

Many of the facilities provided by UNIX to assist C programmers are likely to be aped in other systems. Moreover, the presence of so many useful programming tools under UNIX is likely to provoke a demand, and hence a supply, of equivalent facilities in other systems offering C. So, though this chapter is intended primarily for users operating under UNIX, it should not be regarded as being for UNIX users alone.

First of all, if you are working under UNIX you should seriously ask yourself whether you need to be writing a C program at all. UNIX has many powerful utilities by the aid of which you may be able to achieve your aim with much less effort than you would need to write a C program, particularly if your task involves manipulating text. The shell itself is a powerful programming language, which is superb for manipulating files as single entities. Moreover it can be used to string together commands that already exist, or new ones written *ad hoc* in C or generated with the aid of one of the other utilities, to make powerful file processors. For simple text processing, UNIX has a stream editor sed; while, if you need to treat files as sequences of records, there is a utility with finer resolution called awk.

Two very powerful utilities are lex and yacc. Both are program generators. The former produces a program that will perform specified actions when it detects particular patterns in data presented to it. Although originally designed to generate lexical analysers, lex lends itself to a variety of uses. yacc stands for "yet another compiler compiler". It is more powerful than lex, for it is capable of interpreting a grammar. It would be capable, for instance, of generating a control program, which, presented with a sequence of commands in a special-purpose language, could cause a mechanical device to perform as desired. Both lex and yacc require segments of C to be provided to define actions; but at least they make writing the "front end" of a variety of applications a good deal easier.

9.1 THE UNIX SHELL

The *shell* is the UNIX user interface, and it maintains a number of run-time variables. Most UNIX systems offer a choice of two shells; and some offer more. It is not our purpose here to describe any shell in detail, merely to discuss typical features that are useful to C programmers, and are therefore likely to be aped in non-UNIX implementations of C. One of these is the facility, which we discussed in Chapter 6, for the user to pass parameters direct to the run-time system via the array argv.

The UNIX C compiler may recognise a further shell-like array variable, envp, whose components point to a set of strings of the form "name=value" defining the current operating environment. envp is useful if you want to change the environment from within the object program. There is also a function getenv(name) in the UNIX standard library that is rather easier to use. name in this case is a string; and getenv returns a pointer to the associated value. If you use getenv you may find that you have to declare an external variable

```
char * * environ;
```

which points to the array of environment strings.

9.2 SYSTEM CALLS

The UNIX kernel is well defined by a set of low-level calls that exercise all its functions. These functions are all available to the UNIX C compiler, and the equivalents of many of them may be directly available on other implementations. Several are made use of by the C libraries, which generally offer equivalent facilities in a more convenient form. But some system calls provide things that cannot be obtained from the standard libraries.

9.3 CONCURRENT PROCESSES

One of the things that programmers increasingly want to do is use parallelism. In most computers of course parallelism is an illusion achieved by sharing a single processor in real time. But the illusion does permit programs to be written in the belief that concurrency is really there, often making it possible to use algorithms that are more natural than ones involving only a single control sequence. C does not, like some languages, permit individual statements to be executed in parallel; but UNIX, and some implementations of C, allow the user to create separate processes that will run in parallel.

Under UNIX a new process is created by the system call fork(). This makes a second copy of the memory image of the program's data segment, which then becomes the basis for a second process executing the same program text. The fork function returns a value to each of the two processes. To one it returns the process identification number that the system has assigned to the other. To this process however it returns zero. The first process is then known as the *parent* process: the other is the *child* process. They can be distinguished in the program by a test on the number returned by fork(), thus

```
if (fork())
      {program text for parent process}
else
      {program text for child process}
```

A process normally terminates when control "falls off" the end of the program text. Alternatively it can be made to terminate itself prematurely (commit suicide) by executing the system call exit(status). status is an integer, the last 8 bits of which can be made available to the parent process for identification. exit performs certain clean-up operations such as closing files and flushing buffers. Since a child process inherits the whole environment of the parent process, such a clean-up can be embarassing. It is usually better, therefore, to use the alternative system call _exit(status) which omits the cleanup. exit may be called by an original (parent) process created by a shell command. In this case, the status is passed back to the shell, appearing in the shell variable status.

Since parent and child processes normally cooperate on a single task, it is usually necessary to synchronise them so that, for example, the parent does not try to use a file before the child has finished writing it. The system call wait(pstatus) suspends a process until one of its children executes an exit. pstatus is a *pointer* to an integer. The system eventually sets it to point to the status returned by the next exit executed by a child of the waiting process. There is no distinction between children of the same parent. The first exit to occur releases the first wait. If an exit has already been executed before the wait, then pstatus is set immediately, and there is no waiting. The concept of forking and synchronisation is illustrated in the diagram below.

What fork does is create a second process identical to the first, i.e. a *clone*. This is not quite what is wanted. Of course you can write your program to include separate text for the parent and child to execute; but what you probably want in reality is for the child to have a completely different identity from the parent, doing its own thing, quite independently. The system call exec(name), where name is a string corresponding to the legal name of an executable file, causes the executing process

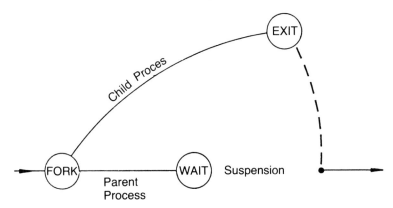

to be overlaid by text from that file, and transfers control to its entry point.

You can also pass arguments from the newborn child process to the program it invokes. To do this, use the call execv(name, argv), where argv points to an array of string pointers terminated with a NULL, enabling arguments to be passed in the manner described in Chapter 6. Some systems have an alternative execl(name, arg1, arg2, . . . , argn, NULL) for use when the number of arguments is known in advance. Details differ between shells and between versions of UNIX.

9.4 PIPES

One valuable feature of UNIX is the facility for creating pipes. A *pipe* (or *pipeline*) is a buffer that can be written to by one process and read from by another. The system call pipe(fd) creates the buffer and assigns two file descriptors, one for each end of the pipe, to the two-item array fd. A file descriptor in this sense, sometimes called a *handle* is an integer, being in most systems an index to a table containing buffer details for all open channels. The system opens fd[0] for reading and fd[1] for writing.

Having created the pipe, the process then forks, when fd is copied to the child process as part of the parent environment. The two processes can then communicate by using the two components of fd for writing and reading respectively. We saw however in the last chapter that the C subroutines that perform reading and writing use not integer indices but pointers to refer to files. This incompatibility can be resolved either by converting the components of fd with the address operator, or by using the system calls read and write in place of the C subroutines fread and fwrite.

9.5 SIGNALS

Another mode of communication between processes is provided by *signals*. The signal mechanism was originally devised so that one process could terminate, or "kill", another. The system call kill(pid, sig) sends the (integer) code sig to the process designated by the process identification number pid. A process may send a signal to itself.

The system call signal(sig, function) primes a program so that if it is sent the signal code sig then the designated function is called. The signal is then said to be *caught*. If signal is not called within the program, then the latter takes some default action that depends on the nature of the signal. The action reverts to the default as soon as a signal has been caught; and has to be re-primed by another call to signal.

Most signals originate in the operating system, and are caused by abnormal events such as peripheral incidents and program errors. A list of these can be found in a header file signal.h. Some signals cannot be caught, and must be handled by the operating system. An example is SIGKILL (code 9), which terminates the process. An alternative to this is SIGTERM (code 15), which may be caught by a process and so lead to a cleanup procedure before exit.

9.6   THE COMPILER

The principal C-specific programming tool obviously is the compiler. In UNIX this is called by the command cc, which is followed by one or more file names. This command accepts a sequence of named source *or object* files, compiles those that require compilation, and links all the modules together, incorporating the standard library. The final object code is written to a file a.out, which is also made executable. Source file names processed by cc must end in .c, and those of precompiled object files in .o. Thus for example

        cc this.c that.c theother.o

cc will also accept files written in assembler, whose names must end in .s.

cc has a number of options. We note a few of those most commonly used. The option −o filename causes the load module to be placed in the named file instead of the default a.out. Option −c suppresses the linking phase of the compiler, leaving the compiled module, or modules, in files with names the same as those of the sources but with .o substituted for .c. Because this option suppresses linking, unresolved external references are not treated as errors. It is used therefore during separate compilation for preparing precompiled modules.

The option −O invokes an object-code optimiser, which can sometimes have an appreciable effect on the speed of the target code. −w suppresses warning diagnostics, leaving only genuine errors. −I followed by a directory name causes files named in quotes <in contrast to angle brackets> in #include directives to be sought first in the named directory. An option of the form −Dname or −Dname=value causes the name to be treated as if it had been defined by a #define directive. If the value is omitted, a default of 1 is assigned. −Uname causes the name to be undefined even if it is defined in the program text.

The UNIX link-loader, which is called automatically by cc, is ld. This combines separate modules, resolves external references, and searches libraries. It has several options, some of which cannot be specified when it is called via cc. The output is placed in a.out unless the option −o name has been used to name another output file. The option −M produces a simple load map.

9.7 LIBRARIES

Libraries are treated differently from other modules by the linker, since only those functions are loaded that are explicitly declared external in some other module, or are required by other external functions. The linker treats any filename ending in .a as referring to a library (a standing for "archive"). It also expands any option of the form −lx into either /lib/libx.a or /usr/lib/libx.a. The compiler automatically attaches the option −lc when it calls the linker, so as to get the standard library; but other libraries must be quoted either explicitly or in the abbreviated form −lx in the compile command. This applies even to libraries that have been supplied with the compiler, such as the mathematical library, −lm.

If you want to collect some of your own functions into a library, then you will find commands to help you among the UNIX utilities. The archiving command

    ar r archive-name namelist

links all the files in the name list into the archive. The option r, shown here, causes files already in the archive to be replaced (i.e. updated) if they have names that duplicate names in the list. An option t causes the contents of the archive to be tabulated. There is also a "verbose" option v, which causes ar to report continuously on what it is doing.

Archives do not necessarily become libraries. Those that do should be further processed by a utility ranlib, which prepends a table of contents _.SYMDEF, to give the loader rapid random access to functions that have been passed over, but are later found to be required after loading files that call them. If you want to reorder the items in a library so that they can be loaded in strict sequence, despite dependence of one file upon another, then you can use utilities lorder and tsort. The former establishes the dependences, and the latter performs a topological sort in consequence.

9.8 lint

Because C is such a permissive language, the compiler will accept as syntactically correct many constructions that do not quite mean what the programmer intended. The UNIX compiler therefore comes with a program verifier lint, which looks for possible points of weakness. lint does not produce object code, so it generally runs faster than the compiler; but it performs lexical and syntax analysis like a compiler. It also looks for possible non-portable features in a program, such as constructions dependent on order of evaluation, or, what is permitted by several compilers, mixing integer and pointer types. It reports on unreachable statements, names declared but not used, and function return values that are ignored.

lint has a number of options for including or suppressing particular checks, or for checking portability to particular systems. It also accepts the −D, −U and −I options of the compiler. It is a good idea to run a new piece of program text first through lint before attempting to compile it; and to use lint as a final check for portability on a working program.

9.9 DEBUGGING AIDS AND OTHER TOOLS

The standard debugger in later versions of UNIX is dbx; though many installations still have the earlier version, sdb. For the debugger to work, it must be supplied with a symbol table so that the user can refer direct to variable and function names during execution. A symbol table is normally attached to the output if ld was used for linking, unless it has been stripped off by use of the option −s or −S; but this table tends to include labels generated by the compiler — to mark the ends of loops for instance. Compiler labels can be removed with the option −X. There is normally no symbol table in the output from cc, but it can be retained by using the option −g in the compile command.

The command dbx a.out gives the user full control over the execution of the program in a.out. He can set and delete breakpoints at specified lines in the program; run the program between breakpoints or between function calls and examine, and if necessary reset, the values of variables. There are other facilities too, such as the opportunity to trace function calls, and the ability to single-step over a specified number of lines or function calls. You can remove the symbol table when the progam has been made to work, and thereby save space, by using the command

    strip program_name

The symbol table can be printed out by the utility nm. Names are sorted alphabetically.

Although not strictly a debugging aid, a *profiler* gives information that can indicate whether or not a program is running as it should. A profile is a table giving a count, possibly among other things, of the number of times each function has been called, and the amount of time spent in each. Its primary purpose therefore is to help the user to decide how he may reorganise his program so that it runs faster. For a profile to be accumulated, the compiler must include code to count function calls. This is achieved by calling the compiler with the option −p or −pg. The compiled program can then be run under the control of the profiler. The command prof a.out causes the program to be executed and automatically produces the desired statistics. The difference between compiler options −p and −pg is that the latter permits the use of a more extensive profiler, gprof.

It is also helpful to have a printed program that is properly laid out with the text indented at the start of every new block. To save you the trouble of having to do this manually when preparing or amending the program, many versions of UNIX provide a C "beautifier" cb that processes program text in this way. The programs in the next chapter have been processed by cb. Finally, the command size will print the size of the code, initialised data and uninitialised data segments for any object module or program.

9.10 PROJECT MANAGEMENT

The command make searches the working directory for a file called makefile or Makefile. This should contain a list showing the interdependence and method of compilation of every module making up a job. For instance a file containing

```
wordsworth: william.o dorothy.o windows.s stringfns.a
    −cc −o wordsworth william.o dorothy.o windows.s /
            stringfns.a
william.o: william.c strings.h mystrings.h
    cc −c william.c
dorothy.o: dorothy.c strings.h ctype.h mystrings.h /
            graphics.h
    cc −c dorothy.c
stringfns.a:
            ranlib stringfns.a
```

might show that a word-processor called wordsworth depended upon two C modules, an assembler module, and a specialised library, together with certain #include files.

A call to make when the working directory contains the above [Mm]akefile performs automatically all the compilations necessary to update the target and object files for wordsworth, taking into account all changes to source files since the last call of make for this target. make has several options. If you do not want to use the name [Mm]akefile, then type

```
make −f another.name
```

The option −n inhibits updating, but prints the commands that would be needed to achieve it. The option −i causes make to ignore any commands in the makefile that do not succeed.

The proper use of make can save time and effort when a project runs into more than one or two modules; though it is unlikely to prove adequate for large projects involving several programmers, since it does not automatically preserve earlier versions of source files. However, there is nothing to prevent you from having several makefiles for the same project.

Chapter 10

Programming Examples in C

The programming examples given in this chapter are intended to illustrate techniques discussed in chapters 6, 7 and 8. They have deliberately been kept simple to avoid confusing the issues. Consequently they are not offered in any way as finished pieces of software; though they could act as a basis for any reader who seeks to build upon their foundation. They have been tested on a VAX under UNIX BSD 4.2, and (*mutatis mutandis*) on a Sinclair QL using the Metacomco/Lattice C compiler.

10.1 ACKERMANN'S FUNCTION

Ackermann's function is a cliché; but it is useful for several reasons. One is that it makes quite a good benchmark. Another is that it illustrates recursion rather interestingly. It is a recursive function that cannot be expressed in a simple *primitive recursive* scheme. The full definition is:

```
A(0, n) = n + 1
A(m, 0) = A(m−1, 1)
A(m, n) = A(m−1, A(m, n−1))
```

In this example, the recursive definition is not translated immediately into C. To get a proper idea of how the function is evaluated, you need a trace. This is provided as a macro using conditional compilation, which can be invoked by defining a constant tracing. A convenient way to do that under UNIX is to compile using the command

```
cc −Dtracing ackermann.c
```

With the Lattice compiler the option −dtracing is included for the first pass.

```
#include <stdio.h>

/* macro for tracing intermediate values */
#ifdef tracing
#define T(i,j,k) \
        k = A(i,j) ; \
        printf("A(%d, %d) = %d \ n", i, j, k)
```

139

```
#else
#define T(i,j,k) /
        k = A(i,j)
#endif


A(m, n)
int m, n ;
{
        int x, y ;
        if (m==0) return n+1 ;
        if (n==0) {
            T(m-1,1,x) ;
            return x ;
        }
        T(m, n-1, y) ;
        T(m-1, y, x) ;
        return x ;
}


main()
/* test for Ackermann's function */
{
        int p, q, n = 0, x ;
        while (n != 2) {
            printf("Type two arguments \ n"} ;
            n = scanf("%d, %d", &p, &q) ;
            /* check number of arguments provided */
            if (n=2) {
                T(p, q, x) ;
                printf("Ackermann(%d, %d) = %d \ n", p, q, x) ;
            }
        }
}
```

10.2 A FASTER ALGORITHM

This second version of Ackermann's function illustrates arrays. It incorporates a speed-up technique in which an array is used to hold values already computed, so that they can be obtained again by a simple look-up.

```c
#include <stdio.h>

/* macro for tracing intermediate values */
#ifdef tracing
#define T(i,j,k) \
          k = A(i,j) , \
          printf("A(%d, %d) = %d \ n", i, j, k)
#else
#define T(i,j,k) /
          k = A(i,j)
#endif

#define maxn 1000 /* table width, depth is 4 */

/* table for holding earlier values */
int A_table[4][maxn] ;

A(m, n)
int m, n ;
{
          int x, y ;
          x = (m<4 && n<maxn)? A_table[m][n] : 0 ;
          if (x>0) return x ;
          if (m==0) return (n<maxn? A_table[0][n]=n+1 : n+1) ;
          if (n==0)
          {
              T(m-1,1,x) ;
              return (m<4? (A_table[m][0]=x) : x) ;
          }
          T(m, n-1, y) ;
          T(m-1, y, x) ;
          return ( m<4 && n<maxn? (A_table[m][n]=x) x) ;
}

testack()
/* test for Ackermann's function */
{
          int p, q, n = 0, x ;
          while (n != 2)
          {
```

```
            printf("Type two arguments/n"} ;
            n = scanf("%d, %d", &p, &q) ;
            if (n=2)
            {
                    T(p, q, x) ;
                    printf("Ackermann(%d, %d) = %d/n", p, q, x) ;
            }
        }
}

main()
{
        int p, q ;
        /* initialise table */
        for (p=0; p<4; p++)
                for (q=0; q<maxn; q++) A_table[p][q] = 0 ;
        for( ; ; ) testack() ;
}
```

10.3 SIMPSON'S RULE

Integration by Simpson's rule is a well known technique. The example enables us to illustrate the use of real numbers in C, the use of the mathematical library, and how to pass a pointer to a function. The compile command to be used under UNIX is

```
cc simpson.c −lm
```

You can test the effect of varying the number of intervals by passing intervals as a parameter to the program (see 10.6 for the technique). If you want to try different functions, compile them as separate modules (see 10.4)

```
#include <stdio.h>
#include <math.h>

#define intervals 10
#define pi 3.14159265358979

double simpson(pf, from, to)
double from, to, (*pf)();
/* integration by Simpson's rule */
{
```

```
        int j;
        double h = (to-from)/intervals/2;
        double odds = 0.0, evens = 0.0, x = from;
        for (j=0; j<intervals; j++)
        {
                x += h;
                odds += (*pf)(x);
                x += h;
                evens += (*pf)(x);
        }
        return ((*pf)(from) + 2*(odds + odds + evens) −
                (*pf)(to))*h/3;
}


main()
/* tests Simpson's rule by comparing sine with integral of cosine over two
regions */
{
        int j;
        double step = pi/intervals, x = 0.0;
        for (j=0; j<=2*intervals; j++)
        {
                printf("%10.6f,%10.6f,%10.6f,%10.6f/n",
                        x, sin(x), simpson(cos,0.0,x),
                        simpson(cos,−pi/2,x));
                x += step;
        }
}
```

10.4 A SORTING PROGRAM

This example introduces structures and pointers to structures. It also
gives us an opportunity to illustrate the linking of two modules. The
module heapsort.c contains the sorting process proper which is independent of the data to be sorted. The algorithm consists in partially ordering the data in the form of a binary tree as it is presented, so that by
subsequent inorder traversal one gets the data in well-ordered form.
The nodes of the tree form an array; and each node corresponds to the
data item with the same index, which is held in a separate array. The
algorithm holds the index itself in the tree node, though this is not
strictly necessary. The module heapsort.c has no access to the data

proper, but uses three external functions: getitem, putitem, and keycomp, to manipulate and find all it needs to know about it.

All direct references to the data are contained in a second module sort_data. The version of sort_data provided here generates some arbitrary test data by using pseudo-random numbers. It could be replaced by any module handling real data items and providing the three functions needed by heapsort.c. The maximum number of data items to be sorted is given in a header file sortdefs.h. The UNIX command for compilation is

```
cc heapsort.c sort_data.c
```

```
/* header sortdefs.h */

#define dim 100


/* module heapsort - - the sort program itself */

#include <stdio.h>
#include "sortdefs.h"

extern keycomp(), getitem(), putitem();

struct heap_node
{
        int index;
        struct heap_node *left;
        struct heap_node *right;
}
heap[dim];

insert(n, p)
int n;
struct heap_node *p;
/* add nth item to be sorted into the tree pointed to by p */
{
        if (keycomp(n, p->index))
                if (p->left == NULL) p->left = &heap[n];
```

```
                    else insert(n, p->left);
            else if (p->right == NULL)
                    p->right = &heap[n];
            else insert(n, p->right);
}


put_tree(p)
struct heap_node *p;
/* print contents of tree pointed to by p in inorder */
{
            if (p != NULL)
            {
                    put_tree(p->left);
                    putitem(p->index);
                    put_tree(p->right);
            }
}


main()
{
            int j;
            /* read data and build tree */
            for (j=0; j<dim; j++)
            {
                    getitem(j);
                    heap[j].index = j;
                    heap[j].left = heap[j].right = NULL;
                    if (j) insert(j, &heap[0]);
            }
            /* output sorted tree */
            put_tree(&heap[0]);
}


/* module sort_data provides an array of simple data to test a sorting
module */

#include <stdio.h>
#include "sortdefs.h"
```

```
/* shorthand macro */
#define p datastore[n]

/* definition of data item */
struct item
{
        float first;
        char second;
        int third;
} datastore[dim];

getitem(n)
int n;
/* read next item into location n of datastore */
{
        int j = rand();
        p.first = (float) j;
        p.second = j & 127;
        p.third = j;
}

putitem(n)
int n;
/* print item n of datastore */
{
        printf "%f %c %x \ :n", p.first, p.second, p.third);
}

keycomp(m,n)
int m, n;
/* returns true if item m of datastore sorts before item n */
{
        return datastore[m].third < datastore[n].third;
}
```

10.5 SIEVE OF ERATOSTHENES

Eratosthenes' ancient algorithm for enumerating the primes is a cliché
too. We use it here to illustrate memory allocation in C. As each
"shovelful" of primes is "sieved out" by the algorithm, we claim more

memory space to accommodate the next shovelful. Thus we have no need for advance knowledge of the number of primes present in the number range we have chosen.

The shovelfuls are chained together by using the last item as a pointer. Thus the item itself is fairly complex, being the union of a structure and a pointer. It is given a typedef name P for convenience. The example also shows how a pointer that is type-defined by means of a cast can be indexed as an array. The function calloc() sets the memory area to zero; and we have assumed (possibly non-portably) that this also sets the pointer to NULL.

```c
#include <stdio.h>

#define shovelful 512 /* chosen to match disc block */
#define toobig 5000 /* for a reasonably short execution run */

typedef union Q
{
                struct
                {
                        long twice_value;
                        long next_multiple;
                }
                N ;
                union Q * next ;
} P ;

P * primes, * primes0 ;

sieve(p, n, size)
P * p;
long n;
int size;
/* seek multiples of n in shovelful pointed to by p and of length size */
/* sieve function body */
{
                int j, sieve_out = 0;
                for (j=0; j<size; j++)
                        if (n == p[j].N.next_multiple)
                        {
```

```
                    p[j].N.next_multiple += p[j].N.twice_value;
                    sieve_out = 1;
            }
        return sieve_out;
}


main()
{
        long n = 3;
        int last_prime = 1, sieve_out = 0;
        /* allocate memory for first shovelful */
        primes = primes0 = (P *) calloc(shovelful, sizeof(P));
        printf("2 3 ");
        primes[0].N.twice_value = 6;
        primes[0].N.next_multiple = 9;
        /* test successive odd numbers for primacy */
        while ((n += 2) < toobig)
        {
                primes = primes0;
                sieve_out = 0;
                /* for all complete shovelfuls */
                while (primes[shovelful-1].next != NULL)
                {
                        sieve_out |= sieve(primes, n, shovelful);
                        primes = primes[shovelful-1].next;
                }
                /* last shovelful */
                sieve_out |= sieve(primes, n, last_prime);
                if (sieve_out) continue;
                /* otherwise a new prime has been found */
                if (last_prime == shovelful-1)
                {
                        /* allot another shovelful - last is full */
                        primes[shovelful-1].next =
                            (P *) calloc(shovelful, sizeof(P));
                        last_prime = 0;
                }
                /* output new prime and put in shovel */
                printf("%d \ n", n);
```

```
        primes[last_prime].N.twice_value = n + n;
        primes[last_prime].N.next_multiple =
            n + n + n;
        last_prime++;
    }
}
```

10.6 SIMPLE TEXT JUSTIFIER

In this example we illustrate the string-handling capabilities of C. We also illustrate the use of argc and argv to pass options from the command to the program. The "raw" command takes text from standard input, cuts it into lines of length at most 70 characters, and delivers it to standard output. Option −A causes both left and right margins to be adjusted. Option −L permits line lengths other than 70 to be selected. A typical command under UNIX might be

```
a.out −A −L 60 < textfile > outfile
```

```
/* Options are −A   adjust both margins
                −L n line length n, default 70,
                       max. 100
*/

#include <stdio.h>
#include <ctype.h>
#include <strings.h>

static space_left, ll = 70; /* line length */

char sin[30]; /* input buffer */
char sout[100] = " "; /* output buffer */

int getword()
/* get a space−delimited word from standard input */
{
        int j;
        /* ignore leading spaces */
        while ( isspace(sin[0] = getchar()) ) ;
        /* look for next whitespace */
```

```
            for (j=1; j<30; j++)
                    if (isspace(sin[j]=getchar()))
                        {
                                sin[j] = ' ';
                                sin[j+1] = '\ 0';
                                return j;
                        }
}


adjust()
/* pad sout with extra spaces from the left */
{
                int j, k;
                while (space_left > 0)
                    {
                        for (j=0; j<ll−space_left; j++)
                            if (sout[j] == ' ')
                                {
                                        for (k=ll; k>j; k−−)
                                            sout[k]=sout[k−1];
                                        /* ignore further spaces */
                                        while (sout[j] == ' ') j++;
                                        if (− −space_left < 1) return;
                                }
                    }
}


main(argc, argv)
int argc;
char * argv[];
{
                int k, doadjust = 0;
                /* interpret options */
                while (− −argc > 0)
                    {
                        if (!strcmp(*++argv, "−A")) doadjust = 1;
                        if (!strcmp(*argv, "−L") && argc)
                                ll = atoi(*++argv);
                    }
```

```
/* input text */
space_left = ll;
while (!feof(stdin))
{
        if ((k=getword()) > space_left)
        {
            /* output line if not enough room */
            space_left++;
            sout[ll+1] = '\0';
            if (doadjust) adjust();
            puts(sout);
            sout[0] = '\0';
            space_left = ll;
        }
        /* move word from input to output buffer */
        strcat(sout, sin);
        space_left -= (k+1);
}
/* flush buffer */
puts(sout);
}
```

10.7 SIMPLE LETTER PROCESSOR

This example illustrates how to handle files. A standard letter, stored in file "letter", is to be adapted for sending to several recipients whose names and addresses appear on file "addresses". Copies of the letter, preceded by each of the names and addresses in turn, are accumulated on a print file called "mail". Insertion characters, defined as backslashes, embedded in the letter enable the copy process to be halted periodically while the operator types, for a particular recipient, suitable text insertions. The full text appears on the terminal, where a beep warns the operator that another insertion is required. Each insertion should be terminated with a newline, which does not appear in the output. The final output is line-filled by a simple wraparound technique when the line exceeds 50 characters, but the right margin is not justified.

```
#include <stdio.h>

#define newpage ' \ 14' /* printer specific */
#define insertion ' \ \ "
#define wrap 50
#define beep '\ 7' /* system specific */

static linecount = 0;
char next[70];
FILE * addresses, * letter, * mail;

output(c)
char c;
/* send characters to output, inserting newlines appropriately */
{
        if (linecount++ > wrap && c == ' ') c = '\ n';
        if (c == ' \ n') linecount = 0;
        return (putc(c, mail));
}

more_text()
/* copy next piece of letter; return true if insertion required */
{
        char c;
        do
        {
                if ((c = getc(letter)) == insertion) return 1;
                putchar(output(c));
        } while (c != EOF);
        return 0;

}

main()
{
        char c;
        /* open files */
        addresses = fopen("addresses", "r");
        letter = fopen("letter", "r");
        mail = fopen("mail", "w");
```

```
/* get and display next address */
while (fread( (char *) next, sizeof(next), 1, addresses))
{
        fwrite( (char *) next, sizeof(next), 1, stdout);
        fwrite( (char *) next, sizeof(next), 1, mail);
        linecount = 0;
        /* get letter and amend it */
        while (more_text())
        {
                putchar(beep);
                while ((c=getchar()) != ' \ n') output(c);
        }
        putchar(putc(newpage, mail));
        rewind(letter);
}
fclose(mail);
}
```

Appendix 1

Syntax Diagrams for BCPL

program:

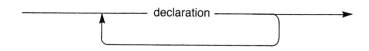

declaration:

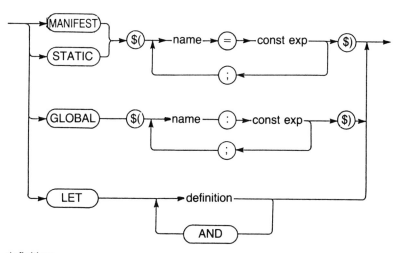

definition:

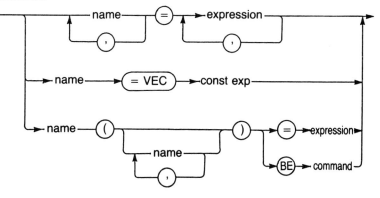

const exp:

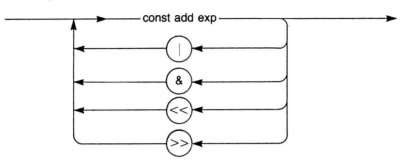

const add exp:

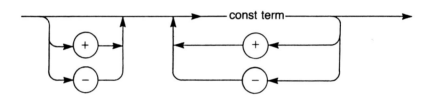

const term:

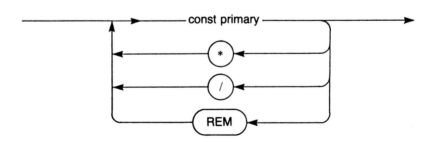

const primary:

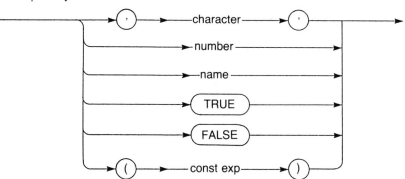

expression:

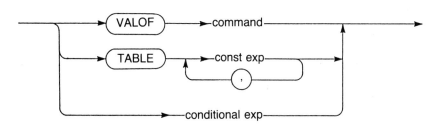

conditional exp:

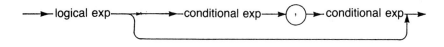

logical exp:

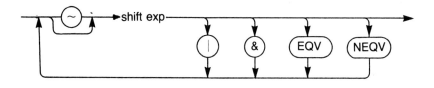

shift exp:

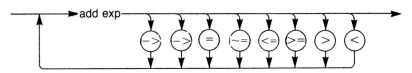

add exp:

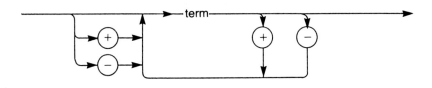

term:

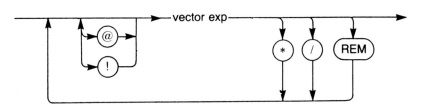

vector exp:

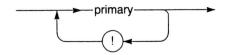

primary:

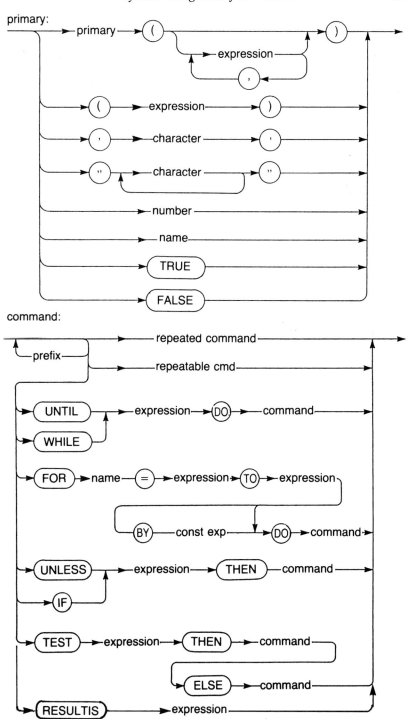

command:

prefix:

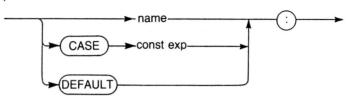

repeated command:

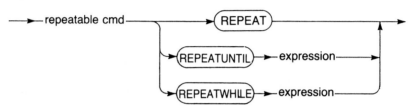

repeatable cmd:

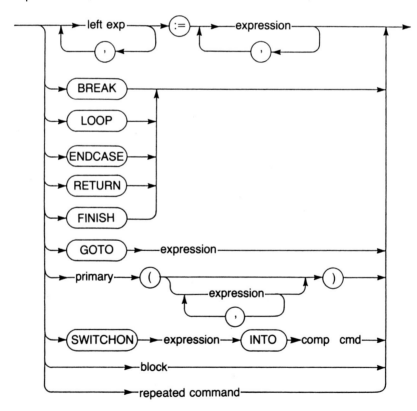

left exp:

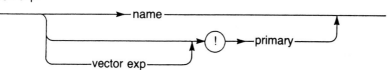

comp cmd:

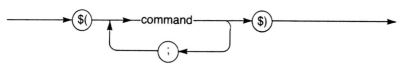

block:

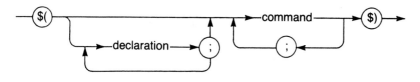

Appendix 2

Syntax Diagrams for C

program:

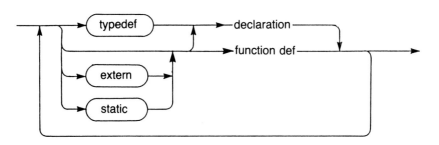

declaration:

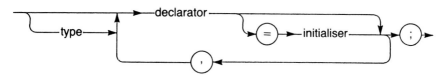

initialiser:

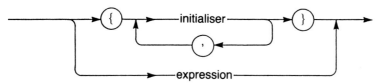

declarator:

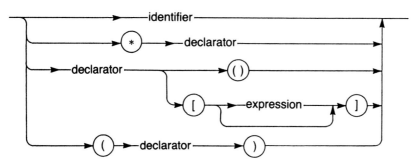

function def:

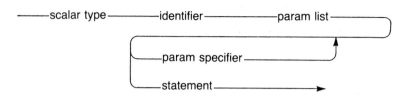

param list:

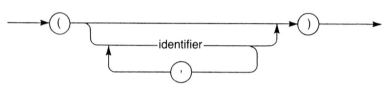

param specifier:

scalar type:

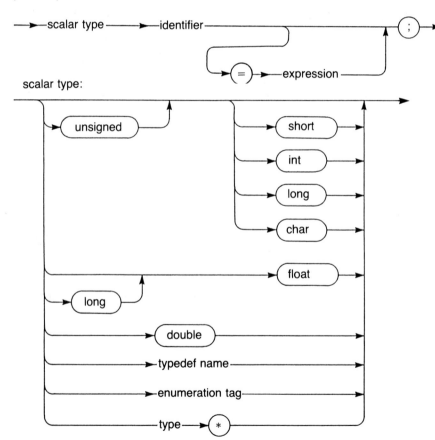

type:

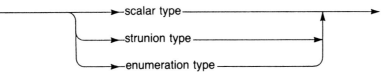

strunion type:

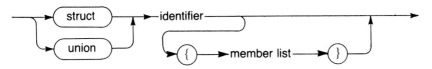

member list:

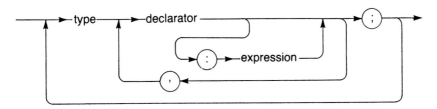

enumeration type:

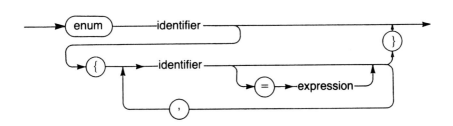

Appendix 2

statement:

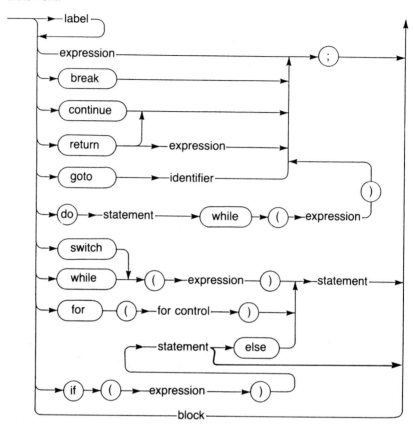

label:

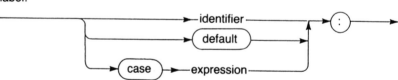

for control:

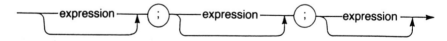

block:

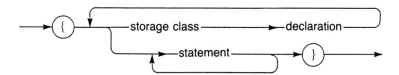

storage class:

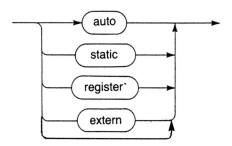

expression:

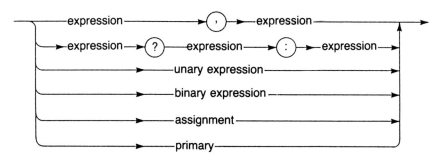

unary expression:

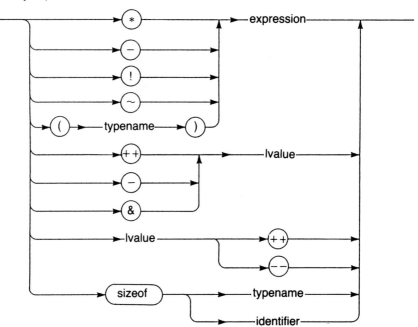

lvalue:

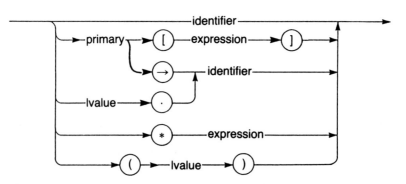

typename:

type ━━━▶ abstract decl

abstract decl:

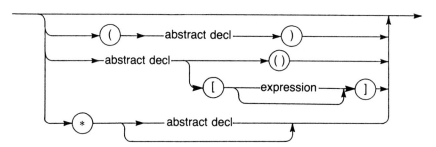

binary expression:

————►expression————►binop————►expression————►

binop:

$* , / , \% , + , - , >> , << , > , < , >= , <= , == , != , \& , \wedge , | , \&\& , ||$

assignment:

————►lvalue————►asgnop————►expression————►

asgnop:

$= , += , -= , *= , /= , \%= , >>= , <<= , \&= , \wedge= , |=$

primary:

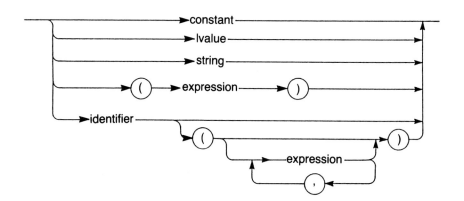

Index

171